# What People

"Scott Whitaker has neatly consolidated the vital truths and fundamentals about what I call 'the membership concept,' which I have used for my own fortune and countless clients. His advice is drawn from solid, successful experience, not theory. To be a member, it must mean something and that meaning must be systematically reinforced. Scott knows this."

—DAN KENNEDY, Author *NO BS* book series;
Founder, Magnetic Marketing

"Scott Whitaker is an outside-of-the-box thinker with a world of experience helping people create high-level membership programs. He's a strategic thinker in launching and selling. I consider him a great friend and mentor, and have leveraged much of his knowledge to create greater levels of success in my businesses. Every time I launch a new membership, I reach out to Scott for his insights."

—MIKE AGUGLIARO, Founder
FuDogGroup.com

"I met Scott about a year ago at a time when we were really looking at our coaching business and seeing how we could optimize it, how we could provide more value to our members, and how we could get our offering right to our customers. I can't recommend him highly enough for any coaching business that wants to take their business, and really their life, to the next level."

—CLINT SALTER, Founder
Dance Studio Owners Association

"As the founder of several membership programs, I am always looking for new books on the topic. Finally, there is an ultimate guide. I cannot recommend this book more highly. Scott is brilliant and tells you everything you need to know about how to grow your membership."

—KIM WALSH PHILLIPS, Founder
Powerful Professionals

"Scott Whitaker is wicked smart when it comes to planning strategy and tactical execution of all aspects of membership programs. From member indoctrination to renewal to ascension to selling and pitching, you will gain huge value from working with Scott. His ideas have easily increased my coaching revenue by multi-seven figures for my company. He verified and clarified things my team has been telling me for how to change and improve what we do, but it took Scott to help me see the wisdom of changing things up, so we can deliver much more value and make much more money long term from our members. Hire Scott today! You won't regret it."

—KRIS MURRAY, Founder
Childcare Success Company

"During a simple lunch meeting, Scott showed me how to immediately add six figures to my membership and how to quickly get new members with what I was already doing. If he can do that over lunch, think how much more he can do for you through his book."

—OLI BILLSON, Founder
www.OliverBillson.com

"Through Scott's simple plan and his proven experience, we were able to create a new level of membership that will significantly increase our monthly recurring revenue. Scott helped us identify underutilized membership assets we already had and capitalize on these, which went a long way to creating our new level of membership. He has a unique ability to develop programs, working backward from the desired outcome, and giving you the step-by-step execution plan!"

—MICHAEL ROZBRUCH, CPA
Founder of Roz Strategies

# HIGH-TICKET
# COACH

The F.A.S.T.
System
to Create,
Launch
and Sell

a High-Ticket
Membership
Offer

## SCOTT
## WHITAKER

Year of the Book
135 Glen Avenue
Glen Rock, PA 17327

Hardcover ISBN:     978-1-64649-251-0
Paperback ISBN:     978-1-64649-246-6
E-book ISBN:        978-1-64649-247-3

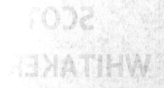

*To my loving wife, Kelly,*
*for believing in me and*
*trusting that together,*
*we could launch F.A.S.T.*

# CONTENTS

# PREFACE

I've had the privilege of launching many memberships. And the thing about launching is that you only get to do it once. Of all those memberships that have been launched, there are "two firsts" that stand out most.

Before launching Membership Multipliers, I was serving as the President of Church Leader Insights with Nelson Searcy. It was during that time that I was able to help grow the membership from 72 members to over 3,172, making it the largest coaching organization for pastors of churches.

But the "first launch" really started in a hotel lobby in Southern California. For a couple of years, I'd been hearing Nelson say that he wanted to launch a membership that would reach more pastors than ever. I saw his content and ideas of what he would coach them on. We had even talked through strategies of how to get people to sign up.

It was in that hotel lobby, while we were sipping coffee, that I told him, "It's time!"

I challenged Nelson to finally launch what had been brewing in his mind for years... to fulfill the calling to impact so many more.

Before anyone knew what a membership site was, before Facebook and Twitter are what they are now, before Instagram even existed, we set out to launch a membership and do it F.A.S.T.

And within 30 days, we launched that membership and gained over 200 members. They paid for their membership before we even delivered the first coaching session.

Fast forward a few years. I decided to step down in my role as President of Church Leader Insights. Like Seinfeld, I was on top and I decided to change paths so I could help other coaches get members. I had already built the largest coaching organization in its niche and I wanted to help others do the same.

That's when the "second first" launch occurred.

It was over the kitchen table when my wife, Kelly, asked me, "What's next? What's your plan?"

You see, I had no email list, no address book of contacts, no database to begin marketing to, no marketing funnels, no lead magnets, no products to sell.

Like many of you reading this book, all I had was a collection of thoughts in my journal, "my unique genius," just waiting to be shared with others.

I looked up at my wife and said, "All I need is this computer, and I can do it all over again." And from that day forward, I set out to launch my own high-ticket membership offer and do it F.A.S.T.

In just five weeks, I sold my first $5,000 high-ticket offer.

And since then, there have been multiple launches of my own membership levels, as well as launches of my members and private clients. I've had the privilege of helping all of them generate a combined nine-figures in membership revenue and tens of thousands of members.

That's how I got the name "Membership Multiplier."

I share these "two firsts" with you for a few reasons.

1) **This isn't some theory** on launching a high-ticket membership offer. This is a proven process that I've used multiple times. If you follow it step-by-step, you can launch, too.

2) **Make a commitment**. Follow the process. Don't skip ahead. Don't glance over what you're reading. Get out a notebook and pen and take action. You owe it to the people you desire to serve with your membership to make it the best membership in your niche.

3) **Make a commitment to do it F.A.S.T.!** There's something about speed. Speed will cover a multitude of mistakes. Too many memberships get stuck on the launch pad due to overthinking and doubt. Speed will also attract the right people to your membership and help you build momentum.

4) **Surround yourself with those who believe in you**. In both of these stories I just shared, there were people who believed. Nelson believed it was possible. My wife believed it was possible.

I believe in you! Sure, I may not know you, but I want you to know that this book was written with you in mind. It's written to the person who has the desire to serve as many people as possible. It's written to the person who has a unique way of serving others and is best accomplished through a membership business model. It's written to the person who is going to make a multiplicative impact and who desires to be compensated for it.

Let's launch F.A.S.T. together!

# INTRODUCTION

It's time to finally launch your high-ticket coaching offer – and launch it *F.A.S.T.*

Here's something I already know about you... there have been a lot of obstacles that kept you from actually launching your coaching program and getting it off the ground.

Some of those barriers include:

- Identifying your right-fit prospects and really knowing what they desire

- Knowing how to attract those prospects and build a relationship with them

- Acquiring your first member when you don't have any members at all

- Getting more prospects to say, "Yes! Sign me up!"

- Trying to locate your next members while still coaching your current members

- Scaling your business without creating a monster that constantly demands your time and attention

Those are just a few. And this book will help you overcome these barriers in every way possible.

Let's dive in.

## What It Means to
## Launch Your Membership F.A.S.T.

The F.A.S.T. acrostic is the framework to creating and implementing your new membership.

**Important**: You may be tempted to skip ahead. Don't do that! You'll miss out on the foundational principles necessary for your long-term success. This is a proven framework that has consistently launched highly lucrative coaching programs (including mine).

In the chapters that follow, we'll dig in to each segment of the F.A.S.T. Launch formula.

### F – FIND OUT WHAT YOUR AUDIENCE DESIRES TO JOIN

Through work with countless clients, I have learned the single most beneficial step you can take is to discover both what it is you can provide your audience and what your audience truly desires.

There's nothing like setting out on an adventure like this, yet wondering whether people will actually want to join your membership. This system will finally give you confidence that people will flock to your membership.

### A – ATTRACT YOUR RIGHT-FIT MEMBERS

You may say, "Hey, I want to make my membership broad so I can attract as many people as possible." Avoid this costly mistake.

Instead, only go after those prospects who are your right-fit members. And that should be a very specific, narrow niche.

## S – SCALE YOUR SALES WITHOUT SELLING

There are a couple of things to understand about sales.

First off, as someone who desires to launch a coaching program, you have probably erred on the side of wanting to focus more on *delivering* your coaching than on selling it. Perhaps you're not even really all that interested in *selling* your membership.

Well, you're also going to learn a process so you can make and scale sales without feeling like a salesperson.

There really is no worse experience than to try to sell somebody on a membership, because no one's actually interested in buying "membership." It isn't a product. It isn't a resource. It isn't a course. It's a *community* that you're providing your members.

You won't want your members to feel sold. You want them to truly desire to raise their hand expressing interest in your membership.

And then last, we're going to learn how to...

## T – TURN UP THE VOLUME AND DEMAND

Once you're getting members and people to actually join your coaching program, how do you turn it up? How do you create demand for even more people to join?

Before we get started, let me ask you an important question...

## Where Do You Want to Be One Year from Now?

If you were to take out a journal right now and write down your dream, I want you to dig deep and tell me where you want to be one year from now.

Be realistic, especially if you're starting from scratch.

In order for this F.A.S.T. Launch System to be a success for you, think about how many members that would look like.

And if we're going to talk about members, we also need to talk about revenue. This process will help you think about launching your coaching program at different levels of monthly investment.

Perhaps you will start out pricing at a couple hundred dollars per month. Or you might be aiming for a membership at $297 or $497 a month.

If you're considering a high-ticket membership offer, I'd suggest starting at $997 a month or higher. Some of my clients even provide memberships at $1,500, $2,000, and above. Personally, my high-ticket membership offer is currently at $5,000 per month. (Yes! You read that right. $5,000 per month, and unlike some gurus out there, I actually have people who gladly invest that every month. I practice what I preach!)

Your pricing and revenue are going to be specific to you. But what do you desire those revenues to be?

And just as important, what would all this mean for you personally? How would that revenue affect the number of vacation days you take?

Maybe you're looking at coaching as a side job, and want to give up your main job when this can become your primary business. What would it mean for your personal income, for your ability to travel, for fulfilling your purpose?

In my experience working with business coaches, I've learned that the best really do want to expand their impact in the lives of the people who join their membership. What would that mean to your ability to fulfill your purpose?

## Where Are You At Right Now?

You might be saying, "I don't have any members," or you might have picked up this book because you never really launched your coaching business. Perhaps you already have started gathering members for your membership. Or you might provide courses as part of your business, but now you're looking to create an ongoing membership for those who complete the course.

Even if you have zero members right now, that's fine.

How much profit would you like to earn from your business?

What kind of impact would you like to see happen in the lives of your members?

As you consider these questions about where you desire to be one year from now versus where you are right now, you also have to ask yourself this question...

## What Roadblocks Stand In Your Way?

What roadblocks stand in the way of getting from where you are to where you want to be?

A lot of people set out by saying, "Here are my goals. I want to launch a membership. Here's where I'm at right now, and over there is where I want to be one year from now."

But they never consider the roadblocks that are in the way.

I want to help you overcome those obstacles, but in order to do that, first you've got to identify what they are.

Maybe it's *uncertainty,* driven by a lack of knowledge. Likely you're just unclear of how to go about all of this. If that's your roadblock, we can now identify it and conquer it as we go through this book.

Maybe your roadblock is *fear*. Perhaps you're worried that even after reading this book you still won't launch. Or if you do launch, it won't get off the ground and only a few people will sign up for membership. Perhaps you're worrying about things like, "What do I tell my spouse? My family? What would I look like out on social media?"

All sorts of fears can come into play.

Maybe you have the fear of being perceived as an *imposter*. It's called "imposter syndrome." Let's identify it, let's call it for what it is, and let's knock it out and get rid of it so those fears no longer hold you back.

You might also question whether people are willing to pull out their credit cards and actually pay for a high-ticket coaching offer...

I'm certain the answer is *yes* (both to whether you're questioning this, and what their answer would be)... because if you are already making an impact in the lives of others, they're probably waiting for you to provide them the next opportunity. Plus, I'm going to show you a **proven process to make sure that you do get members.**

One of the lessons I've learned in leading membership businesses and growing my own high-ticket coaching program while being an entrepreneur is that the best way to conquer these uncertainties... the best way to conquer these fears... the best way to conquer this question of "will people actually join?"...

...is to take *massive action*:

- First, make a commitment that you're going to go through this book all the way to the end.

- Second, make a commitment that you're going to take massive action and you're going to make it happen.

Here's another profound question...

## If Those Roadblocks Were Removed, What Then?

If you say, "Well, this is where I'm at today... and this is where I desire to be one year from now... and here are the roadblocks that are in my way..." then let's say we remove those roadblocks—you and I, during our time together. Would you still be able to get to where you want to be?

You see, some people self-sabotage because they fear their own success. I definitely don't want that to be you.

With those roadblocks removed, would you still be able to get to where you desire to be? Chances are you'd be able to get *further* than where you thought you would be.

One of my greatest joys would be to hear from you a year from now, after you launch your membership, and hear you say, "I am actually further ahead than where I thought I would be when I first started!"

## The F.A.S.T. Launch Framework

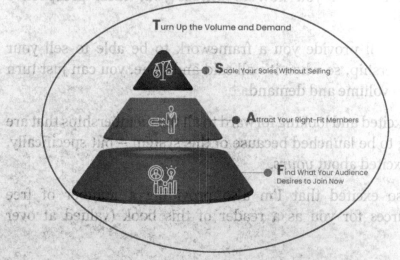

Turn Up the Volume and Demand

Scale Your Sales Without Selling

Attract Your Right-Fit Members

Find What Your Audience Desires to Join Now

This is how we're going to craft your high-ticket offer, build your membership and scale your sales... and do it *F.A.S.T.*

- The bottom of the triangle represents "Finding what your audience desires to join now" – that's got to be the foundation you build upon.

- After that, we're going to "Attract those right-fit members" to join your membership.

- And then we're going to "Scale your sales without selling" so that you can lead a membership and not sound like a salesperson when it comes to providing membership for your people.

- Finally, that circle on the outer edge is all about "Turning up the volume and demand."

We're going to work on the foundation first, starting at the very beginning to uncover your unique genius and activate it so you'll never be in doubt as to what you can provide your members.

Then, once you have that confidence of "this is what I can provide" and "this is what they actually desire to join," we'll go about showing you how to attract your ideal prospective members.

Next we'll provide you a framework to be able to sell your membership, so when it's all said and done, you can just turn up the volume and demand.

I'm excited and looking forward to all the memberships that are going to be launched because of this system – but specifically, I'm excited about *yours*.

I'm so excited that I'm also providing a number of free resources for you as a reader of this book (valued at over

$675.97!) All you have to do is go to www.FastLaunchCoach.com to get your free resources. Plus, you'll be able to join my community and get answers to your challenges.

If there's ever a roadblock, if there's ever a question, just reach out directly. My goal is to help you launch your membership and do it *F.A.S.T.*

# Part 1

# **F**ind Out
## What Your Audience
## Desires to Join Now

# 1 | UNCOVER YOUR UNIQUE GENIUS

In this chapter, I'm going to take you through a number of steps to uncover your unique genius.

As a coach or consultant you have a "unique genius" to help others. This systematic process will help you identify all the skills you already possess to help others. You will never again have to doubt or guess at what you're going to provide your members as part of your coaching program.

Regardless of whether you've been following me for a while, or if this is our first time going through this together, I want you to know that I practice what I preach and I literally repeat this process *every single year.*

Why? Well, first it's because I'm constantly learning new things. And second, my members continue to have new needs and new desires.

By going through this process, and later repeating it, I am able to help my members get what they want and need... this year and in future years. I want to help you be able to do the same for your members by teaching you a proven system to make it possible.

I'm going to ask you a series of questions, so grab a notebook or open a new blank document on your computer. You will need to utilize what you find from this process. It's important that you write things down, so you never have to guess what you're going to provide your members.

Feel confident... all this work that we do on the front end is going to relieve a ton of stress on the back end.

A good S-Y-S-T-E-M saves you *Stress, Time, Energy,* and *Money.* And the system I give you next will save you that stress, time, energy, and money from having lost members or wondering what you can provide to them and when.

## Your Content Catalog

We will talk more about the "Seven Membership Multipliers," but for now, know that your Content Catalog is actually the most important of them, especially when launching your brand-new membership.

Your catalog consists of *everything* you can provide to your members – and not just what you can provide now, but also what you *could* provide sometime in the future.

You see, there are some things you can provide immediately to your members if they were to sign up tomorrow, but there are others you might be able to develop over time.

As your members begin to pay you, you might become more willing to spend the time necessary to develop that content or resource or product, whatever it may be, for your members. Therefore, it's not merely what you can offer right now, but it's also what you could potentially do in the future.

These questions are important, because they really do lay the foundation for the experience of your members.

## What Are You Passionate About?

I like to ask this question, first and foremost, because nobody wants to create a membership around something they're not passionate about.

I'm passionate about *membership.* I'm passionate about helping you expand your influence and grow your audience and gather those people inside a membership or coaching program.

What are you passionate about?

I want your membership business to revolve around your passions, because I've found that when it's revolving around your passion, you actually develop a sense of purpose.

So what things are you passionate about? Write those down now!

I've had people go through this experience and say to me, "Well, I thought I was going to start a membership for *these people*. But after you asked me the question about what I was passionate about, I realized that I was actually passionate about *these other people* over here. And after I started going down that pathway, I discovered I could create an entirely brand-new coaching program over there. And it would be something that I'm truly passionate about."

For example, Wendy Weber came to me wanting to start a coaching program. I asked her about the membership she wanted to start and how she would help people. She began to tell me all the ways she wanted to help people with their health and wellness.

However, when I asked her, "What are you most passionate about?" she lit up and told me about all the ways she's helped parents who have a disabled child. Being a parent of a disabled child herself, she had a passion for helping others.

All of a sudden, there was a sense of purpose. By taking Wendy through this process, she uncovered all the ways she has already been helping others and all the ways she could serve even more parents through her coaching program.

You see, just like Wendy, you've developed plenty of skills and knowledge around things that you're *not passionate* about. But by understanding the answer to the question of what you *are* passionate about, you will likely discover that you have additional skills and knowledge focused specifically around that passion.

Next...

## What Are You an Expert At?

I've always loved to ask this question, because in all humility, most people don't like to consider themselves experts. But what are you an expert at?

You see, I do believe you're an expert. I believe we all have an area of expertise. So what are *you* an expert at?

Write down this statement and fill in this blank:
I'm an expert at _____.

There's something that happens in your mind when you actually write down, "I am an expert at" and fill in the blank.

For me, I'm a membership expert. I'm an expert at helping people build, sell, and increase retention and renewals inside their coaching program.

What are you an expert at? If you were to gather your close friends, your family, or people that you've had an impact on, what would they say you are an expert at?

## How Are You Helping Others
## Achieve What You've Achieved?

You might start thinking through things like: "I was able to teach on this one topic" or "I was able to deliver on this," or "If I was invited to speak right now, I could deliver a seminar on this subject matter because I've been able to help others achieve it."

What kinds of things do people actually seek you out to help guide them to do?

(I hope you're not just reading through this. You should be writing down the answers and creating a catalog of everything you could provide for your members.)

Before I created and launched Membership Multipliers, I had leaders of other membership businesses contacting me, asking me to come in and consult with them on their membership. There I was, just growing my own membership at the time – totally focused on growing a coaching program to help pastors. We started with just 72 and grew to over 3,000 members.

When these other membership leaders noticed what I had accomplished, they said, "Hey, can I hire you for a day?" And so, they started paying me to come in and work with them on their business.

Adams Hudson was my very first client. We had just finished a two-day mastermind with Dan Kennedy (yes, Dan Kennedy was one of my mentors) and Adams said to me, "I'd like to hire you to come to my office and consult with us on our membership program."

Adams eventually sold his business and wrote me a letter, saying, "I want you to know that during that day of consulting that I hired you for, we were able to put some things in place that enabled us to get multiple more – multiples on top of multiples – more than what we could have ever sold our business for."

He went on to say, "I owe it to you."

I didn't realize in that moment that I would one day venture out to start my own membership to help coach other membership businesses. I was so focused on the membership at hand that I didn't know there would be that opportunity... like right now, where through this book I've come alongside to help you.

However, I soon realized that not only had I personally grown a membership to be the largest in its niche, but I was able to help others do it as well.

How about you?

You might be saying, "Scott, I don't know that I've been able to help others yet." Well, if you had the opportunity to help others, what would you be able to provide them?

> "Your guidance and coaching were invaluable. I'm proof positive that a membership program has real, calculable, closing-table value that goes far beyond the empty echoes of '...a really good reputation.' Memberships are worth money today, every month thereafter, and then they multiply again when you go to sell your business. In my case, the value created was well into 7 figures. Thank you for your continued guidance."
>
> —ADAMS HUDSON, President, HudsonInk.com

## What Services Do You Provide?

When I first started my coaching business, I only provided consulting services. But now I also provide masterclasses, courses, events, high-ticket membership offers, and all sorts of services that I've been able to add to my catalog over time.

What's really great about your Content Catalog is that when you go through this process every year, you can examine the things you weren't doing – or weren't able to do – in the very beginning, and create additional offerings for your members.

What services do you already provide? You might consider consulting services. What other services could you provide if given the opportunity?

Some of these options might include "Done For You" or "Done With You." The former is easy to understand, but the latter is where, just like in this book, you take your members through the process, coming alongside them to have them do it with you.

What services can you provide?

## What Products or Courses Do You Provide?

You might not have a product or a course yet, but if you do, jot those down. If you aren't in a position where you already have a product or course, if you were given the opportunity, what products *could* you offer?

If you were able to carve out a couple of hours in one week, what product could you create? If someone said to you, "I'll give you $1,000 right now for a course," what course or courses would you build?

### What Do Your Members Need?

Interestingly enough, while writing this section I was checking my email and somebody reached out to me and said, "Hey, listen. I'm not sure if this particular program is right for me or not. You see, I lack the confidence in being able to sell."

Well, well, well... that was interesting.

First off, it was interesting that someone would be willing to actually confess that lack of confidence within themself. But

I've come to realize that my members *do* need confidence in selling their memberships and high-ticket offers.

I never would have realized the value of mindset work back when I was first starting out to help people grow their memberships. I thought I'd be working on their skills, but I've come to find out that more and more, once we upgrade people's mindsets to help them believe they *can* make an impact, everything else gets easier.

For example, if you as a coach are going to sell a high-ticket coaching program, you can't stutter when you state the price. (I know this too well, considering I've had a speech impediment.)

What do your members need? Maybe they need confidence as well. What do you have that could help them grow their confidence?

## What Internal Problems Do Your Members Face That You Can Offer a Solution To?

Again, confidence would be one option – it's definitely an internal factor that people have to deal with. But what other internal problems do your members face?

Something mentioned earlier was that people often have the problem of feeling like an imposter, like they're somebody they're not, or even a fraud. In my experience, that's definitely not the case. Instead, it's just insecurity.

Do your members struggle with such insecurities or fears?

What are those internal problems that your members face that you can offer a solution to?

## What External Problems Do Your Members Face?

An external problem one of my clients had was that their members needed the support of a spouse in order to participate in the membership.

I wouldn't call a spouse an "external problem," but it was certainly an outside factor because it meant that in order to sell this membership, their prospects would have to get the buy-in and approval of a spouse. That's definitely an external factor.

What external factors do your members face? Are they relational? Are they financial? Does somebody else make the decision about how money gets spent?

What external problems do your potential members face? Is it a knowledge problem? Is it a skill that you might teach them? What prevents them from growing in that skill?

Again, I encourage you to write these answers down. Capture your thoughts in the moment as we're going through this process.

## What Do Your Members Need,
## But Don't Know They Need?

Without a doubt, I know one of the things my members need – but don't *know* they need – is to raise their prices. I'm just blown away by how little many of them are charging for their memberships.

And I know what you're thinking... "Well, I hope you're going to talk to me about how much I should charge for a membership." Yes, we'll talk about that soon enough...

But some of my clients have been charging the same price for their memberships for 10 years. Prices have gone up everywhere else, inflation has happened, yet nobody ever told them that they too needed to raise their prices.

## Other Ways to Add to Your Catalog

If you're having some difficulty putting down answers to these questions, or you're finding out that your catalog isn't as full as you would like it to be, here are some sources you may want to check out.

- www.AnswerThePublic.com lets you type in questions about your specific subject matter and will let you know all the things that people are asking about around that topic on the internet. You'll see all sorts of questions pertaining to it. Also, you'll see what people are searching for when they go to Google.

  These search terms are invaluable. Some of those topics might help you understand the internal problems people are having, as well as their external problems, through questions they want to get answered. All of this information will help you learn and discern what you can provide to your members.

- Facebook Groups: Search Facebook for groups that contain your right-fit members. No! Don't SPAM the group or try to leech off members from the group. Instead, observe their comments. Read the questions they're asking. What are their struggles? What are their victories?

  Let me say again, your primary purpose is to observe and learn. Nothing else! That Facebook Group doesn't belong to you.

- www.Amazon.com: I love going to Amazon and checking out the book section. You can pull up well-known authors who are experts in the specific field that you're going to be building a membership around.

Here's how you do it. Search for the "top 100 books" around your topic. Then scroll down to the comments and review section. Check out the comments people are saying and read the reviews they are leaving. Readers reveal how that book helped them overcome a problem or helped them to see a solution or helped them to experience a transformation. (You'll also find a lot of great sales copy in those comments as well.)

All of a sudden, you can discover exactly what your audience desires to join.

Some of these authors, by the way, have spent thousands and thousands of dollars on research. Yet you can just piggyback off their hard work that they've already put in by writing that book.

Just read the comments. You share the same audience, so why not? The answers are already out there.

- www.Quora.com: Quora may not be applicable for every membership, but for some, there are threads and discussion boards taking place around a particular topic that will be of infinite use to you. Why not read some of those discussion boards?

  Just beware. There are a lot of negative discussion boards, but you'll find people encouraging other people out there as well. Consider how you can create services, products, or courses around the problems your market needs to solve.

- www.Medium.com: Search for articles that people are writing about your particular subject. You might also find that you could build a relationship with the person who wrote that article and get them to provide content for your members.

There are many online sources available to you. Back in 2006 when I helped start my first membership, we didn't have all the expansive resources of Facebook, LinkedIn, and social media. We couldn't go to Amazon or AnswerThePublic.com or Medium.com to quickly find out what people were wanting.

To get to know our audience, we had to connect with them on a personal level. You can still do the same... but now it's so easy! You can simply go out on Facebook and ask a question.

Also don't be afraid to meet people outside of your sphere of influence. All these sources are available to you and make it super easy to uncover your personal genius and to discern what offerings you can provide your membership.

Here are a couple more questions to consider...

## What Content Do Other People Have That You Can Provide?

As just mentioned, there are authors on Amazon and Medium.com... and these experts would love to be interviewed. If you were just to ask them questions about their article or book, you could expose these authors to your members, and likewise introduce your members to those thought leaders.

One of my clients hired experts to come in and share their area of expertise with his members. This was a great way to deliver high value to his members while relying on the expertise of others to help members get the outcomes they desired.

Even if you don't know these experts personally, you can still reach out to them and ask if they will share their knowledge. Many will do so without even being paid!

## What Content Can You Surprise Your Members With?

In this step, I'm talking about surprise content – just something that will help out your members in the moment.

This is something that comes down to live events and online events like perhaps a bonus masterclass. For example, when the pandemic struck, I used Facebook Lives consistently as surprise content for our members to try to help them even further.

What content can you surprise your members with? Maybe it's a quick online event or additional masterclasses. What can you do?

## Write This All Down

If you haven't been writing things down, you're actually doing a disservice to yourself.

I don't want that for you.

Creating your Content Catalog is all about taking away the guesswork and never having to guess at what you're going to provide your members. Plus, it's going to relieve stress, free up your time, give you more energy, and keep your members from quitting.

Which means more money in your pocket.

Write down your answers and create that Content Catalog.

I do this every year. I repeat my own process, building my Content Catalog, expanding it in all the ways I can further impact members.

Write it all down.

Then, when in doubt, visit those websites to see what people are saying. While you're out there, you might actually find a new topic of discussion or new content that you can provide for your members.

This whole process will give you not only a catalog, but also Intellectual Property you can provide to your members. And when you don't personally have the expertise, there are other people who can bring it to you.

Susan Berkley, founder of Great Voice Company, went through this exact process. She hired me for a VIP Day and we mapped out three high-ticket coaching programs using the Content Catalog exercise.

In the picture that follows, you can see giant post-it papers hanging on the wall behind us where Susan listed all the content that she could share as part of her unique genius.

**VIP Day with Susan Berkley, founder of Great Voice Company**

Go through this process for yourself, write it all down, and never guess again at what you're going to provide your members.

---

Access your free copy of the
Content Catalog exercise

**www.FastLaunchCoach.com**

---

"Going through Scott's process has been an incredible experience. I mean, he dug deep into my business. We got into numbers. We got into creating memberships. And I can see from here going forward how much money we can make. This has been a real dream of ours to implement a membership in our business. It's the one way to really get the kind of revenue jump that we've been looking for. And with Scott's help. We could not have done this ourselves. So, I really, really recommend Scott. You're in the right place."

—SUSAN BERKLEY, Founder, GreatVoice.com

# 2 | CATEGORIZE YOUR UNIQUE GENIUS CONTENT

Let's continue our journey into your content as we uncover your unique genius.

This content is already inside of you, ready for you to give birth to it – almost in the sense of giving birth to your membership. This content is also what will fuel your launch. It is the rocket fuel your membership needs.

Let's dive in.

In the previous chapter we went through a process to design your Content Catalog. Now I want you to go back and pull out everything you've written down, either in your notes or on your computer. Next we are going to talk about how to categorize your content for your members' success.

## Content Categories

You might ask, "Scott, why should I categorize my content? Why do I need to do that?" Well, here's what I've found...

As you look over your Content Catalog, I can guarantee there are some items in the list that you are more passionate about than others.

There are certainly things I get more excited about delivering to my members than others. Even though I know my members need to learn about "ascending their members" – moving members to progressively higher levels of service – I just don't get as excited about it as I do about "marketing to get more members." But my members still need to learn about "ascending their members."

In this step of categorizing your content, we're making sure your members can get the outcome and the success that your coaching program promises them. We're making sure they will get what they need from your membership.

Therefore, instead of it being a program about what excites *you* – what *you* want to teach, what *you* want to provide – it instead needs to be built around what your members need to succeed.

That's why you have to categorize. As we develop your catalog and your categories, you will be able to provide the best, most well-rounded experience for your members.

If you're still not sure why you need to create categories, think of it this way...

Let's say you're going to a gym to purchase a membership. When you visit, they have a bunch of treadmills. Only treadmills. I mean, this gym is *full of treadmills*. You say to yourself, "I don't want to run on the treadmill today. I want to lift some free weights."

So you say to them, "Hey, I thought I was joining a gym. Where are the free weights?"

Then they reply, "Oh yeah. Well, in this gym, all we do are treadmills."

You don't want that experience for your members. You want to not only offer what you're most excited about, but also what your members truly need and desire.

This is why we categorize.

First I'll show you some categories I've used personally, and from there you get to build your own. There are no right or wrong answers when it comes to these categories.

## Evergreen vs. Time-bound

*Evergreen* content or services are things you can provide regardless of the time of year. It doesn't matter if it's January or the middle of summer, or just before a holiday. Timing doesn't matter at all. You can provide this content anytime. It's evergreen.

*Time-bound* content is specific to a date or season or opportunity. You might say, "Here we are on January 1st. Let's talk about goal setting." This is a time-bound offer unique to January 1st.

Just remember, evergreen content can be used at any time, and time-bound content is for a specific time of year.

## Process vs. Organic

This book, for example, shows you a *Process*. The F.A.S.T. Membership Launch is a systematic process of how to go about launching your membership.

By contrast, something that is *Organic* stems from ideas that lead you or someone else to think differently or take action, but it doesn't include a step one, step two, step three set of directions. Instead, it just happens.

*Organic* content is great when people are joining your membership at different times of year or when their starting points along the journey are different. Your organic category of content can be useful for any member, regardless of season or how long they have been part of your membership.

## Done With You vs. Done For You

*Done With You* means you will do something alongside your members and they will play an active role.

*Done For You*, however, means you will provide a service or product in which the member does not have to be an active participant.

## The Seven Membership Multipliers

Start by thinking about these *Seven Membership Multipliers*, outlined below:

1. **Content**: All of your content falls into categories, including the content you are currently creating as part of your Content Catalog.

2. **Assimilation**: This step is all about taking a new member from signup to becoming fully engaged.

3. **Marketing**: There are two kinds of marketing in this step. The first helps you to get new members, and the second helps you to keep them.

4. **Retention**: Keeping members long-term is all about relationships and results... and giving both to your members.

5. **Accension**: This step is about how you will move members upward and downward in their membership journey.

6. **Strategy**: This step allows you to think strategically about your membership.

7. **Leadership**: You also need to think about giving people the confidence and tools they need to actually succeed at what you are teaching them to do.

As you begin to categorize your content, you get to choose your own categories.

When I first started out, my categories fell into either *Multipliers* or *Accelerators*. Inside the category of Accelerators, I further subdivided my content into Marketing Accelerators, Assimilation Accelerators, and Retention Accelerators. These are tools that help my members *accelerate* the growth of their membership.

But you get to choose your own categories. Here's how you can get started...

## You Need to Be Balanced

There are categories you will likely get more excited about. I actually enjoy the Content category of helping people discover their genius and seeing that light bulb AHA moment go off in their minds. By comparison, my Ascension categories don't feel as exciting to me. But if Ascension only gets paid lip service, then my members will not be able to grow or retain their membership or take those members to new levels. Without that piece, the overall membership would be far less desirable.

Your Content offerings need to be well balanced. You need to utilize *all* the different multipliers in order to provide the most balanced experience possible within the membership... creating a pathway for success and for your members to get the most out of their membership.

So, as you reshape your understanding of what your members need from your membership, are there any additions to your Content Catalog that you would make?

Think about that for a moment.

Is there any Content you previously considered offering for a specific time of year? Or any new Content that would be valuable year round?

Just by adding categories, many times that helps you generate fresh ideas for what you could add to your catalog.

## Let Others Choose the Categories for You

Finally, if you're stuck on trying to figure out the categories you should come up with...

- Revisit www.AnswerThePublic.com and look at all the different categories provided to you right there.

- Go to Amazon.com, look under books in your topic area, then check the sidebar for additional categories of similar books. They've done the work for you.

- Go to Medium.com and seek out people who may have already written articles for the different categories contained inside your membership.

Why not look at what other people have already done? Why not let them be able to help you figure out how to categorize your content?

Again, this is all about creating that best opportunity, that best pathway for your members to succeed and enjoy your membership. Find out what **problems they desire to fix** or troubles they need to **resolve, and then create a well-balanced** membership for them.

# 3 | SCHEDULE YOUR UNIQUE GENIUS

Here comes the fun part.

Now that we've done the hard work of building your Content Catalog and categorizing it, we get to *put it on your calendar*.

If you're just starting out, I understand that you may not even know when your membership is going to launch. That's okay. I'm going to show you the process, regardless of whether you're launching next month or six months from now. That way you'll be ready and have everything laid out on your calendar.

But first I must ask:

## Is There Content that Correlates with the Calendar?

I hope I've already jogged your memory and caused you to do some creative thinking about holidays.

- If your membership is for women, then you might want to consider doing something special around Mother's Day.

- If your membership is specifically for men, you might consider Father's Day.

- If your membership is something that involves getting outdoors, you might consider the summer months.

As I work with coaches in different niches, I help them identify whether there's a cycle inside their calendar. For example, around the fourth quarter of the year, many memberships can make a big marketing push – or host an annual event – to entice new members. You could develop content around that time of year or event.

Perhaps there are months of the year that are naturally slower – where you can make time and space to talk about things that wouldn't normally be on the radar. This could allow your members to gain momentum going into those bigger months.

I've discovered that every niche has some sort of ebb and flow. Content or services can correlate directly with the calendar and time of year. Be sure to take that into consideration when planning your Content Calendar.

## When People Get Charged, Is Something Delivered?

If you're charging people for your membership on the first day of each month, make sure something gets delivered.

I recognize that many will be delivering something – content, products, services – at a specific time even though people might be charged later. I'm okay with content being delivered *in advance* of the customer getting charged.

This isn't meant to be complicated. What I want you to make sure is that there's something already delivered, or delivered at the same time as people are being charged. That way, at no time does somebody make a payment without something having been provided to them.

## Set Regular Deadlines Throughout the Year

Repeat this exercise, because there's nothing like a deadline on the calendar to motivate you.

For example, I created specific deadlines while writing this book – chapter outlines, first draft content, and revisions. The proof that this process works is that you're now holding this book in your hands.

There's nothing like driving toward a deadline, so create deadlines within your own calendar to propel you forward and to motivate you.

As you think about your schedule, will there be something that you will do every week for your members? Will there be something that would show up every month? How about every quarter?

There might be things in your Catalog that prompt you to ask, "Why not do this for my members once each quarter?"

Other content will take place annually. One of my clients holds an annual event just for members, so every year it's part of their Content Catalog.

Create deadlines for your content, resources, and services that you will provide annually, quarterly, monthly, and weekly. Write these dates down in your calendar and do this for every single month of the year. Ask yourself, "Is there something I should be doing this first month of the year? Second month? Third? Fourth? Fifth?"

HOLIDAYS

Don't limit the holidays to just the ones that immediately come to mind. Search online for "January holidays" and you'll get a list that includes at least some you were never aware of before.

For example, January 2nd is World Introvert Day. If your membership serves introverts, then align some content for this time of year that specifically helps them better navigate based on their natural tendencies. Or if your membership serves primarily extroverts, consider offering content to help them better understand their counterparts.

## MONTHLY/QUARTERLY/ANNUAL

If you have content you want to deliver each month, consider what time of the month makes the most sense, and then plan your personal deadlines to be prepared to meet those delivery dates.

For quarterly content, ask yourself what and when you plan to provide it. Will it fall on calendar quarters, or some other division of once every three months? Set dates on your calendar for both delivery and planning time so you can meet your deadlines.

For annual content, start by thinking about the delivery date (or event date, if it will happen in-person or online). Once that date is selected, then consider what needs to be prepared ahead of time.

For example, if RSVPs need to be received by a certain date, when must you send the invitations to your members? If the invitations must be physically mailed, when must you have the files designed and sent to the printer? Add these deadlines to your calendar so you will not be surprised by them later.

## Focus on Your First Three Months

If you are in a position where you have not launched yet, then I suggest you focus on just your first three months. Avoid the overwhelm. Don't worry about trying to prepare an annual calendar yet.

Consider which months will start your launch. Let's say you're going to launch in July. Then plan out July, August, and September. What will you provide in the first month of your launch? What content, products, or services will be part of the second month? And then the third?

Remember to keep writing down your answers to each step along the way!

Start with that first month of launch. What will your members receive immediately? Will other content or deliverables become available all at once, or over the course of a few weeks?

Now continue with the second month. What gets delivered, and when will it happen?

Soon you will have the first three months of your entire membership all mapped out. You're going to know exactly what you're going to provide your members and when.

If you haven't done it already, now is the time to start moving those ideas from paper or digital file into your calendar.

Now you will be able to focus on providing the content you have planned, at the times you have planned them. No more guesswork. No more worries. You can focus on your launch. You can focus on serving your members. All because you know and have a plan.

Guess what happens next?

Once you have a solid picture of those first three months, you will be able to repeat this process as you start planning out the next three months, and then the next three months, and the three months after that.

When you're first getting launched, simply repeat this process every three months until you have a plan for the whole calendar year.

Then each time you plot out the next three months, move those ideas from paper or digital file into your calendar. Also add them to a spreadsheet or some sort of master list. Have a gathering place for both your Content Catalog and your Content Calendar.

Then after a year of delivering your membership, you will have created an entire catalog which you will be better able to leverage the following year!

"Scott was able to give me a lot of awesome clarity, creating different levels of membership programs. I'm so enthused about leveraging the experience I've had and know we're going to create an even bigger impact and bigger contribution by shortening the learning curve of some of the other business owners in our industry."

—DAVE COYLE, Founder
Maverick Drycleaners Marketing

# 4 | FOUR WAYS TO LEVERAGE YOUR GENIUS

Once you've launched your membership and delivered some incredible content, at some point you're going to consider revisiting that same content (or something similar). You will likely hesitate, saying to yourself, "I can't teach that again. I've already taught that. I've already provided that. I've already told them that."

Guess what? It would be doing your members a disservice if you don't provide it again.

## Repurpose Your Content

Let's imagine you just prepared some content for your membership in the form of a handout. You could take that exact same information and repurpose it into a blog post. Or you could teach it live, either online or in-person. Or you could prepare a video.

Why should you repurpose this content? Because if you don't, your members probably won't be able to really *learn* it.

As humans we need to hear and see and do things multiple times before we truly integrate it into our lives. Additionally, different people learn in different ways – so having content that is written is great for some, while others will do better if they hear it. Still other members will need to interact kinesthetically to learn. Therefore, it's your duty to repurpose your content so you can best help your members.

Once you've considered how to repurpose smaller content pieces like articles or handouts, now let's consider the possibilities for content you provide that's of a larger scope.

Let's say you have amassed a dozen articles, or created content that teaches numerous steps or processes. You could:

- Turn it into a masterclass

- Turn it into a podcast

- Take that masterclass or podcast and get it transcribed, and then turn the combined content into an e-book

Once you have your initial content created, challenge yourself to look at each piece of content with fresh eyes. How could you repurpose it over and over again?

Your members need this from you. Don't presume that just because you taught it once, they actually learned it all the first time.

## Recycle Your Content

Along with repurposing, you will also have content that you can simply recycle.

You've already discovered with your Content Calendar that certain content makes sense to deliver at a certain time of year. For me, I know I will present a masterclass each September on how to sell your membership during the holidays. I do this every single autumn because it's always relevant.

Why? Because my members need to know how to sell their memberships leading into the holidays. It's a great time for them to do it, and for us to do it alongside each other where I'm able to do it with them.

We talk about that topic every September and moving through the months that follow. Every element of the content I created for this masterclass can be recycled.

Each January, I try to do something that helps members plan a one-year Content Calendar. I recycle this content every year. But it's not completely recycled. Remember that we're always learning new things... so you will always be adding new things.

I'm constantly gathering new information, new strategies, and bringing that to my members, but you will be able to recycle that basic content over and over.

Don't think that just because you did it last year, that you can't do it again.

## Reframe Your Content

What do I mean by reframe?

Let's say that every January you teach goal-setting with your membership. You have framed it around the beginning of the year.

However, you could take that same content and say, "Hey, it's June already, and we're halfway through the year. Let's plan some goals together and see how you can finish the year strong."

All that is required is to take the same content that was previously framed for January and reframe it for June.

## Resell Your Content

I know that "resell" technically means to sell again, but that's *not* what I'm talking about. You don't sell the same thing to somebody twice.

What I am saying is that there is specific content you will provide to your members that you could also extract and sell to non-members.

Maybe you've been wanting to create a course. Maybe you've been wanting to provide a live training. Why not provide it to your existing members as a great benefit as part of their membership, but then sell it at a ticketed price for non-members?

And don't worry if the non-members will see it again later should they finally become members. Because there's power in...

## Repetition

Let's say that someone joined your membership after you shared a specific piece of content. For example, I taught a goal-setting process in January, but a new member joined in March. They weren't there for the January goal-setting. The first time they're going to hear it is in June. Everything will be fresh and new for them.

But for the member who did hear that message in January and went through that process, don't you think they would still benefit from renewing or adapting their goals in June?

Absolutely.

You will be able to provide continued value for your members by constantly helping them and training them and growing them. And you can do it by leveraging existing content.

In *The Ultimate Sales Machine,* Chet Holmes talks about the power of repetition. After most people go through some initial training, their skill improves... but then it drops off. However, when it does drop off, they're still in a stronger position than when they started.

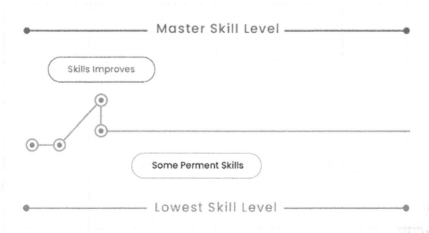

Later, let's say they repeat the same training. Their skill improves, but there's another drop-off and plateau. Still, this second plateau is higher than where they first started... and it's even higher than where it was previously.

Each time the training is repeated, the skill improves. The drop-offs become less dramatic, and more of the skill remains intact.

Through the power of repetition, your members will first learn a new skill, then improve that skill, then eventually acquire the practice and proficiency to master and retain that skill.

As a matter of fact, why don't you make a commitment to yourself that after you finish reading this entire book, you'll go through it again?

Why?

Because you are learning something new here! On the first reading, you will acquire a lot of information and be able to immediately put some of it into action.

But just like what happens with any new skill, as soon as you finish reading this book, some of that knowledge will be lost. When you read through it again, you will internalize more of what you learned the first time, and also notice parts you may not have fully understood the first time around.

The skill drop-off will be less dramatic and more skill will actually remain.

A great thing about this book is that you've got the opportunity to go through it again and again to keep improving what you've already learned. So, why don't you do that?

## Leverage Content in All These Ways

- Repurpose
- Reframe
- Recycle
- Resell

Remember to leverage your content in all these ways so you can help your audience more. Members will benefit from the repetition, and non-members can be introduced to you for the first time as an expert with an existing following.

When you leverage content in this way, you will not only be serving your current members, but you'll demonstrate to prospects the change that is possible through your larger membership program.

Don't buy into the lie that you can't repeat content! No, your members need this repetition from you. It's one of the ways that will make it possible for you to deliver on the outcome and the promise that your membership provides.

# Part 2

# **A**ttract Your
# Right-Fit Members

# 5 | THE ONE THING YOU MUST GET RIGHT

Before we continue, consider a word of warning...

**You MUST follow this process step-by-step and
you MUST get this one thing right.**

The more work you do right now on this one thing – attracting your right-fit members – the better you will ensure that your membership actually gets off the ground, and that you've got the right people on board.

The most important thing you need to remember is this...

## You Do NOT Want Everyone

Please don't skip this step, because you definitely don't want a membership filled with people who are *not* your right-fit members.

The only thing worse than putting out your membership and not getting people to take it is putting out your membership and getting the wrong people to join... because those people will *cancel*. And when you're in startup mode, any cancelation will cause you to doubt yourself.

You'll start doubting your expertise, doubting the content you provide to your membership, doubting whether you should even be doing this. All sorts of doubt will creep in if you fail to attract your right-fit members.

I cannot stress this to you enough. Follow this process step-by-step. Put in the work.

That way, you'll have total confidence that you are attracting your right-fit audience, members who will stay (and not cancel), and that what you're providing them is actually what they desire.

## Right-Fit Members Stay Longer

When somebody is a good fit for your membership, they will stay longer; you'll have a higher retention rate.

## Right-Fit Members Engage More

The people you were truly meant to serve will engage more with your community. They'll engage more with your content, your services, and with all that you are providing your membership.

Take note, however, just because people may not engage in *every* aspect of your offering, it doesn't mean they're not a right-fit member. Introverts tend not to engage socially, or to have a smaller sphere of friends and colleagues. They may sit in the "back row" or in "the corner." But even right-fit introverts will engage with some aspect of your content or services.

## Right-Fit Members Are Excited

I love it when I get to talk to new members and hear their excitement for what's going to happen. You can sense it in their words and mannerisms.

With right-fit members, you almost don't even have to convince them to join. They raise their hands saying, "Hey, I'm interested in joining your membership."

You'll see their excitement almost immediately.

## Right-Fit Members Achieve More

When you have successfully attracted your right-fit members, you will notice that these people achieve the outcome your membership provides.

That's one of your goals, right? You want to help others achieve the outcome your membership delivers.

Right-fit members will achieve it. They'll utilize your training. You'll see their success. They will overcome various challenges. You'll see them bragging about all the things happening inside their life or inside their business – because they're achieving the outcomes that your membership provides.

## Your Right-Fit Members Will Surprise You

Once you launch, you may be surprised at who joins your membership. What do I mean by that?

Well, every now and then it does happen that you discover something you didn't expect about the people who actually join your membership – they're different from who you thought would join.

That's fine. It's possible. It can happen. It doesn't always happen, but it absolutely might.

And if that does happen? Then go after who you reach!

Stop trying to pursue those people who aren't attracted to your membership and start going after the ones you *are* reaching. They're the people who are excited about your membership and who you're going to be best able to help.

Hopefully, you can see the value of getting this right.

In the next step, we'll see how to attract your right-fit members, because I want you to have a clear picture of who you're setting out to attract, while being open to the possibility that if you reach a different audience, you can still pivot and direct your membership toward that audience instead.

# 6 | YOUR SECRET AUDIENCE FORMULA

Now that I have your commitment to follow this step-by-step advice, let's dive into identifying your right-fit members using what I call *"Your Secret Audience Formula."*

Here's what I know:

- You genuinely have a desire to help people achieve their purpose in life, whatever that may be.

Anyone who runs a membership must have a genuine interest in making other people's lives better. Whether that means making their businesses better, or their relationships better, or their financial situation better, you are invested in helping people make positive change.

There are three essential truths when it comes to your membership and which specifically pertain to your right-fit members.

## TRUTH #1: YOUR COACHING PROGRAM IS NOT ALL THINGS TO ALL PEOPLE

Even though there may be another business coach targeting the exact same audience as you, there is a certain segment of that audience who will never join that other person's coaching program.

Even if that audience desires the exact outcome this coach promises, it may be that they just don't feel a connection to that person or to their program.

It will be the same for you. This is why you and your membership can't be all things to all people. You're going to naturally attract a certain group or target audience. And that's okay. Don't bend on this. Recognize that you are best able to serve a very specific group of people.

## TRUTH #2 – IT'S ABOUT ACKNOWLEDGING WHO YOU CAN SERVE BEST

Realizing that you can't serve everyone doesn't mean that all people can't benefit from your membership. In fact, it will be more than likely that they can. By merely acknowledging the reality of who you're best able to serve, the attraction will be stronger, and those outside the tightest parameters will self-select to join with an understanding of the outcome your membership provides.

For example, one of my clients, Lisa Phillips, is the founder of Affordable Real Estate Investments. She coaches people on how to build wealth by investing in real estate. If you were looking to invest in vacation properties, then her coaching program is not for you. If you're interested in flipping houses, then her coaching program is not for you.

Her coaching program is specifically tailored for "African American Professionals to build profitable rental property portfolios." Her members are typically first-generation college educated, first-generation white collar, who have a desire to build wealth through investing in minority neighborhoods.

And if that wasn't specific enough, her coaching offer reaches out to African Americans who want to invest in minority neighborhoods... to help make them a *better community*.

That is her audience.

As a Caucasian male, I'd be welcomed in her membership but I'm not her target market. Even though I'm the one who helped her discover her right-fit member.

Your membership ought to be the same way. It doesn't mean that all people can't benefit. It's just that you will know who you're best able to serve.

TRUTH #3 – THIS ISN'T ABOUT TURNING ANYONE AWAY

Lisa would never turn anyone away from her membership. You're not going to refuse someone from joining yours (although there are a few this may be an option for).

You will more than likely pick up some people along the way who aren't your best-fit members. I'm not suggesting you cancel their memberships, but I do want you to know that you need to be very targeted on who you're best able to serve. This enables you to better sell and serve your members as a whole.

When you have clarity on *who* you're best able to serve, then it provides clarity for *how* to serve them. If suddenly you get members outside of this zone, then you're likely to start questioning yourself, your content, and perhaps even your expertise.

## Your Secret Audience Formula

Now let's identify your right-fit members. As I take you through the questions that make up the formula, I encourage you to pause and really think about your answers so that you can get clarity.

Also, bear in mind that some of these questions will not pertain to every membership. But I'm still going to ask them so that you can open your mind to the potential of who your members might be and understand them better.

## What Do They Look Like?

There is a fitness franchise called Curves. When you think about any health-related service, your imagination immediately begins to fill in certain details. Perhaps you think of obese men who want to lose 50, 75, 100 pounds or more. Or perhaps you think about Schwarzenegger like body-builders who want to carve their muscles with definition.

Well, Curves doesn't serve the entire market. Its membership is only open to women. Based on insight from a friend who is a member, it especially attracts women of a certain age, later in their career. These women have encountered different health issues, and because of that, they now need to lose an extreme amount of weight.

Now, doesn't that paint a picture of what they look like?

## What Do They Wear?

You might wonder why it matters what your members wear? But if I tell you that I like to shop at Nordstrom for my jeans, what does that say about me? It might say that I have expensive tastes. Or that I like the comfort they provide. Or that I like that Nordstrom will tailor them to fit.

That says quite a bit about me, don't you think? So what do your members wear and what does that say about them?

## Where Do They Live?

Your membership may be internet-based. They can live all across the world.

It just so happens that my membership includes people who live in the UK, North America, Australia, and New Zealand – all English-speaking countries.

Where do your members live? Primarily in the U.S.? If so, do they live all across the country, or only in a certain region?

Nail it down.

## Where Do They Work?

First off, this question assumes they work. But do they?

One membership organization I assisted actually targeted retirees. The answer to the question "Where Do They Work" wound up being, "They don't." Yet it still told us something about the right-fit members... They would likely have a fixed income, and that's definitely something to consider when crafting your offer.

So, where do your right-fit members work? And what does that tell you about these ideal prospects?

## Where Do They Shop?

If you know your members shop at Target rather than Bloomingdale's, what does that say about them? Or maybe they order exclusively online for home delivery. Or perhaps they do the bulk of their grocery shopping at Whole Foods.

In each case, you can extrapolate characteristics and preferences based on these shopping styles.

If you consider the shopping preferences your ideal members exhibit, then you will also be able to reverse-engineer creative ways to target new right-fit prospects.

## Are They Married, Single, Divorced, Married Again?

Marital status communicates something important about a person's life circumstances and situation, but it may or may not be relevant in all memberships.

If I told you that my wife and I will soon celebrate our 25th wedding anniversary, what does that say about us?

A membership for 30-something, divorced chess enthusiasts would likely not be a right-fit for me.

If your membership deals with helping people better their relationships or finances, the answer to this question will be critically important to distinguish your ideal prospects.

## Do They Have Kids?

Knowing whether your right-fit member has children – and if so, what age(s) – can also help you discern how to better serve them.

My youngest daughter is about to graduate high school and will soon go into her freshman year of college, and my oldest daughter is now 23.

What does that say about me? I'm entering a different phase of life, because I no longer have young kids. Family dynamics have changed significantly.

Does your audience have kids? What are their ages? And what does that mean?

## What About Grandkids?

My wife and I now find ourselves talking about grandchildren. We don't want it to happen anytime soon, but we look forward to that day when it does.

And this starts to tell you something more about us.

What about your right-fit members? Do they have grandkids? What are their ages?

## Are They Retired?

Earlier we asked, "Where do they work?" Now let's go deeper.

Have your right-fit members retired? If so, do they work in other ways? Maybe they have a part-time job, or are launching a startup. Perhaps they volunteer. If so, what kinds of organizations do they donate their time to?

Are they living off investments or accumulated wealth? Or are they restricted to just a monthly check from Social Security?

Answering these questions gives you a deeper insight into their psyche and who they are.

## What Is Their Income Level?

When you are setting out to attract a certain type of member, knowing their income level is important. It specifically helps you determine how to price your membership, knowing that they'll be able to afford and enjoy its benefits.

## What TV Shows Do They Watch?

Or do they even watch TV? What does this tell you about them?

When you find out someone is attracted to *The Walking Dead* or to *Jeopardy!* that tells you something, right?

There's a certain comradery among those who follow the same show or kinds of movies. Often they share a sense of humor. They also share a vocabulary based around the program's theme or characters.

What TV shows or movies do your right-fit members watch, and what does that mean?

## What Books or Magazines Do They Read?

What can you learn about someone regarding the books or magazines they read?

Do they like fiction or non-fiction? Is there a certain magazine they subscribe to?

Or maybe they don't read.

In my target audience, a really good member is somebody who does read. That's why I've written this book. But if I didn't know that my audience reads, and I didn't have any books, I would be missing out on the chance they could get their introduction to me through one of my books.

(Plus, if they don't read books or magazines, why would you even spend time writing a book?)

What does your right-fit member like to read?

## What Level of Education Do They Have?

If somebody who isn't college educated is the target for your membership, there may be some things that you don't want to talk about... like a system for student loan debt repayment, for example.

And at the same time, if your ideal prospect is college educated, maybe you want to talk in more detail about a specific topic they studied.

What level of education do they have?

## What Kind of Car Do They Drive?

You might say, "Scott, my membership is internet based, so how am I going to know what kind of car they drive?"

Well, if you know my story, you know I led a membership for a pastors' group and helped grow it to become the largest in its niche. And we knew what kind of car a lot of those pastors drove. Most of them were very thrifty. They weren't buying new cars; they were buying used cars. They were also highly conscientious about the kind of car they drove.

Car choice communicates something important about these members.

But let's say I told you that I drive a two-seater BMW Z-4 Roadster. What does that say about me?

Well, you can tell that I'm okay with spending money. You can tell that I'm at a different stage in life because I'm not driving a mini-van, lugging around five kids and all their gear.

What kind of car do your prospects drive?

## What Social Activities Do They Participate In?

If your audience enjoys hunting and fishing and the great outdoors and are members of the National Rifle Association (NRA), you might guess they're also conservative.

Of course this is a broad statement, but stereotypes are *stereotypical* precisely because they represent the typical activities and behaviors of certain groups of people.

You might also consider whether your members are even on social media. Most likely your audience is out there on social media – but perhaps your right-fit members have recently decided to do a "digital-detox" and only log in occasionally.

What social activities do your members participate in, either in the real world or online? And what does that tell you about them?

## Are They Religious? If So, What Religion?

You might know that I am an ordained pastor. Yet I don't call myself religious. Instead I believe I have a relationship with God through Jesus Christ.

You might guess that as an ordained pastor, I hold certain values like integrity and honesty. You can begin to discern other characteristics that are important to me just based upon my religious background.

What about your audience? Are they religious? If so, what religion? Remember that people use a wide variety of terms to express their spirituality.

That might be critical, especially if your prospects are from a different religion than you. I've had people cancel membership once they found out I was a pastor. I'm fine with that. If they were not comfortable with me sharing that story... oh, well. They were not truly my right-fit member.

What about you? What about your prospects? Are they religious?

## What Are Their Values?

This is closely related to religion, but definitely not 100% the same. Values can arise from other factors, including life experience.

Maybe your members came from broken homes and place a high value on the stability of marriage.

Perhaps your right-fit member had an abusive parent and now places high value on programs and organizations that help heal childhood trauma.

Or maybe your right-fit members share values about the treatment of animals, or the land, or indigenous peoples.

What are the values of your members?

## What Political Affiliation Do They Have?

I know society politicizes things way more often than it needs to. But a person's political affiliation still hints at certain deeply held core values.

If your prospects might share a political affiliation, not only will this knowledge enable you to know what to say to them to connect on a deeper level... it can also provide insights into what *not* to say to them.

## Are They from a Certain Geographical Location?

Even if you've only traveled across the USA, you have noticed significant differences in various regions.

From the words people use (like "over easy" vs. "dippy eggs") to the values they grew up with ("don't be late to supper"), geography defines us.

Knowing whether someone came from the city or the country can tell you a lot about them. When someone finds out I was born in Pittsburgh, Pennsylvania, they make assumptions. But then I tell them that I lived in Price, Utah, and later moved to Bozeman, Montana, before ultimately growing up in Savannah, Georgia.

And then when I left home, I lived in Atlanta, Georgia, for a number of years, but then moved to Boca Raton, Florida, and now reside in Charleston, South Carolina.

People will easily make assumptions about each city in that list. Some are as different as night and day. What assumptions do you have about me based on where I lived or grew up?

The geographical location of your prospects (both past and present) can tell you a great deal. Where do your right-fit members live?

## What Are Their Goals?

What would they like to have happen? What would they like to achieve?

If your membership helps people with their finances, that's a very good question for you to answer. What do your right-fit members desire as part of their financial goals?

For some, it might mean paying for a child's wedding, while for others it's purchasing a vacation home or adding an "in-law suite" on their existing home.

If you help people with their relationships, what are their hopes and dreams when it comes to those relationships? What would they like to have happen?

Are they married in an abusive relationship and looking to escape? Or are they single and lonely, looking for a life partner? Or perhaps a spouse has died and now they are looking for companionship.

Understanding their goals will help you frame your membership in ways that naturally attract right-fit members.

## What Are Their Challenges?

People in your membership will almost certainly encounter roadblocks that lie in the way of them achieving their goals.

For some it may be challenges related to technology. Some may share obstacles related to weight loss or disease. Others might experience hurdles involving confidence or self-esteem.

By the way, if you help people to heal relationships, it could be that the spouse is the challenge... yet that person's buy-in is needed in order to join your membership.

## What Are Their Pain Points?

What keeps your prospects awake at night? Are they worried about their health? Or issues facing an adult child? Perhaps they are concerned about losing a job, or changing careers mid-stream.

List all the things that keep your right-fit members awake. These are the pain points they worry about most, and consequently, are the places where you can provide the most valuable solutions.

## What Are Their Objections or Hesitations to Buy from You?

Consider your membership and ideal prospect. You now understand the goals they have, as well as the challenges and obstacles in the way of them achieving that goal. You know their pain points that keep them awake at night.

Now ask yourself, "What are their potential objections or hesitations?"

It could be that they have joined other memberships similar to yours in the past, only to be let down. What does that mean for you? What will you have to do to earn their trust?

First you must help them overcome that hesitation, building their confidence. You've got to give them insight into how your membership is going to be different from what they may have experienced previously.

Next you need to help them understand what your membership offers – how they will benefit from it and how it works – because they've never experienced anything like it before.

## Are They Able to Make the Financial Decision to Buy from You?

Money can be as divisive a topic as politics, but when it comes to building a membership, pricing will be a critical component of your success.

When I launched the membership for pastors, we knew the average pastor could only spend around $99 without needing to get approval from their church leadership. Because a pastor could make this decision on their own, without board oversight, we specifically priced the membership at just $99 per month.

With other higher-ticket offers, we specifically designed a process that would equip prospects to go to their board and ask for approval for that membership.

You might be working with individuals who don't answer to a board or oversight committee, but perhaps they still must get approval from a spouse or other party.

It's important for you to know that, ultimately, your right-fit prospect either has the financial ability to make their own decision, or you will need to equip them to notify others and educate them on that decision as well.

Hopefully, by answering the questions from this chapter, you're now getting a great picture of your perfect member.

---

Download your free copy of
"Secret Audience Formula Action Guide"

**www.FastLaunchCoach.com**

to further identify and attract
your right-fit members.

---

# 7 | ATTRACTING YOUR RIGHT-FIT MEMBER – HIGH-TICKET OFFER CASE STUDY

As a way to help you internalize the process and more easily discern your own right-fit members, I want to share with you a case study.

It's from a private client of mine. Her name is Kris Murray, and she owns The Childcare Success Company. I've been working with Kris for a couple of years now and when we first started working together, we did this very same thing that I'm doing with you. We dove in to identify her ideal prospect and right-fit member.

The Childcare Success Company helps childcare center owners grow their childcare centers and she has three levels of membership:

- *Growth* is a center just starting the process and trying to grow.

- *Freedom* is a center that has been going for a while, but the owner is essentially still a slave to their business.

- *Empire* is a center that is trying to expand – to increase enrollment, pricing, or potentially open additional centers.

Let's consider the right-fit members for each of these levels.

## Growth Membership

We called the membership avatar for this level's right-fit member *Growth Gabby* or *Growth Gus*.

Note that we actually put a name to the right-fit member for the Growth Track, and then we wrote out a description:

> Growth Gabby (or Gus) is in survival mode. She started with a dream to impact children and make a good living for herself. But because she's literally trying to do it *all* – from scheduling staff, doing tours, payroll, licensing, even working in the kitchen and driving the bus – she is 100% overloaded. She has no time to work on marketing her center or reviewing financials, so she's on a treadmill of low to no profit (she may even be *losing* money every month) and has no time to grow her enrollment. She is likely working 60-70 hours a week, not earning the income she dreamed about, burnt out, and lonely. She desperately wants time to work on her business and maximize her enrollment, so she can hire some office help and reduce her stress and overwhelm.

Do you get an understanding of the psychology of what's going on inside this person's mind?

Somebody can read this and say, "Wow, that's me. I just drove the bus this morning to go pick up kids. I had to work in the kitchen this afternoon, process licensing and payroll. Well, I haven't actually done payroll yet. I gotta go do payroll now."

This person can easily see herself on that very same treadmill of low to no profit.

Here's what's key...

After describing this right-fit member, we laid out a *"This is for you"* segment for anyone who can say *yes* to a series of statements.

THIS IS FOR YOU IF...

- You're barely making ends meet and stressed out about making payroll.

- You would give anything for a regular paycheck.

- You're underwater financially and thinking about closing your doors.

- You have moderate to severe under-enrollment.

- Your family or marriage is suffering because you're always at the preschool. (Remember I asked if you understood the marital status of your right-fit member?)

- You're a startup who wants all the tools to be successful, right from the get-go.

And then, with this in hand, my client can tell them exactly what they need most right now.

That's just the first-level growth.

## Freedom Membership

Then we designed a picture and profile for *Freedom Felicia*. Notice that if I'm a Growth Gabby and I start reading this, I would probably say something like: "Well, that's not me, but I sure wouldn't mind trying to get to that point."

> Freedom Felicia (or Fred) has a stable early childhood business, because she already has an admin team in place that runs her school(s). However, she still may provide coverage as a director during emergency times or vacations, and she gets pulled away from her high-payoff projects more than she'd like. She may have a vision for expanding to more locations, or adding more capacity to her current location, but since she still finds herself working more than 40 hours a week and feels burnt out, she's just not sure that dream is in the cards for her. Freedom Felicia needs help with delegation, automation, and systems, so she can *break free* from her business to a greater degree. She also needs great marketing that keeps her school(s) full, to develop consistency in operations across locations, and a growth mindset that will support her on this journey to make a greater impact in her community and the world.

THIS IS FOR YOU IF...

- You have a stable business 60-80% of the time.

- You get pulled in when directors leave, or teacher turnover hits a crisis point.

- You are profitable but still leaving money on the table.

- Company culture and the stability of your team are top issues.

- You need help with delegation, systems, operations, and automation so you can reduce the team's workload.

- You desperately want the business to operate without you so you can break free and get your life back.

Again, what we're trying to do here is to call out the right-fit members. Hopefully you see the value of answering all those questions from the previous chapter now, so that you can truly dial in and understand the issues facing your ideal prospects.

## Empire Membership

Then there's *Empire Ellie.*

Empire Ellie (or Ed) is a visionary leader who has a drive to build an early learning empire. Regardless of your number of locations, you have a big dream for growth, success, or wealth. You likely stand out in your marketplace in terms of quality and/or market share. However, you still question whether your company could run better and more efficiently. You want access to the big ideas and "players" in our industry, and you want a true mastermind group to help you build your empire and avoid costly mistakes. Deal evaluation, financing, wealth-building, advanced marketing, and speed of implementation are what you need most right now. A coach and a peer group of like-minded entrepreneurs will help you go further, faster, and you will feel less alone at the top.

Really consider the implications of that last statement there... *you'll feel less alone.*

By the way, do you think Empire Ellie shops at a different location than Growth Gabby?

I mean, if Growth Gabby is struggling to make payroll and maybe even not taking a paycheck herself, you can bet she's shopping at a different location than Empire Ellie.

THIS IS FOR YOU IF...

- You have a stable profitable business, but you want to go further, faster.

- You have a fast expansion vision such as "7 more schools in 5 years" or "10 to 20."

- You have a desire to build wealth and use that wealth for making a bigger impact and legacy.

- You think to yourself, "Life is okay, but I want something bigger."

- You want to work on an exit strategy or succession plan so you can plot your next move.

- You want Kris Murray on speed dial and the highest level of coaching and masterminding.

Since doing this exercise in mapping out the avatar descriptions for all 3 of her membership levels, Kris has gone from $2.1M in revenue to over $5.7M in revenue – again, just by running through this process and getting super clear on identifying her right-fit member.

Don't get lost in the details that she has 3 levels of membership but maybe you've only got one. Just create the avatar for your membership. If you have more than one level, do it for each level of membership.

Also, don't assume that every level will be attractive to the same person. They're not.

Just follow the process!

## Get Your Launch Trajectory Right from the Start

You want to launch your membership F.A.S.T., like a rocket taking off from the launchpad!

Picture a rocket launch for a moment. That rocket is just sitting on the launchpad, and if its trajectory is off just one degree... by the time it gets into orbit, do you have any idea how far away from its target destination it's going to be?

Those astronauts are going to need a *major* course correction.

But if you get this one thing right with your launch, and you get dialed in on your exact right-fit member, you won't be one degree off – you'll be right on target. Your aim will be perfect from the launchpad.

What I'm trying to help you do here is to make sure you correct that one-degree mistake before it comes back to bite you.

When you're on the launchpad, maybe that one degree doesn't seem like it's a big deal. But I promise that once you're in orbit, it will mean you will be miles and miles off target. So let's perfect your aim now while you're still on the launchpad, to save you major course corrections later.

# 8 | PAINT A PICTURE OF YOUR RIGHT-FIT MEMBER

You just saw an example where Kris Murray learned to describe the mindset of her right-fit members. You saw how she and I were able to practically read the minds of her ideal prospects, creating a description of exactly what that person would be thinking, feeling, and experiencing.

I want you to be able to have that level of insight and understanding for the people you want to attract to your membership. Invest the time right now to fill in that description, just as we did in the last chapter.

First, decide if your right-fit member is gender specific. Is your membership for men, women, or both? If both, do those members still have the same fears and feelings?

Next, I want you to come up with a "This Is For You If You Can Say YES" statement. Pull out your notes from answering the questions in Chapter 6 and ask yourself, "Who is this membership really for?"

**This Is For You If You Can Say YES...**

Maybe you need to go back and re-read the case study. Feel free to model Kris Murray's framework. Just swipe it. I mean literally! Just swipe what she wrote and rewrite it, then craft it to make it your own.

I never want you to start from a blank screen. That's why I shared the case study with you first, so you can get this picture painted in your own mind. Now I'm asking you to paint this picture on paper.

I want you to write 5-6 statements that say: "You're a right-fit member for my membership if you can say *yes* to most of these statements..."

Pause for a moment and write down those statements.

## Here's How You'll Use This...

Now let me tell you how you will leverage those statements to get more prospects, memberships, and sales.

First off, you will be able to write your emails, your sales page, your sales letter, your postcards, and direct mails... everything, *right to that person*. You will know them so well that when it comes time to write an email, you'll be able to pull out this painted picture and write your email directly to your avatar as if they were a real person you've known for a very long time, because you know them on a deeper level. You will be able to speak directly to your own Growth Gabby, Freedom Felicia, or Empire Ellie.

When you send a message, you'll start by saying something like:

"Hey Felicia, ..."

Next, you'll just start writing out your message. And you'll be able to craft it in such a way that it's personalized.

You're going to be writing to their hurts, their wants, their needs, and their desired outcome.

One of the worst things you can say on your membership sales page is that "you're going to get a membership site." That's not what anyone wants. That's not what anyone needs. That's definitely not someone's desired outcome. Nobody joins a membership to get a membership site.

Instead, they want to know, "What will that membership site provide for me?" And that's where you'll say:

> *"You have at your fingertips instant access to find the resources and tools you need – so that in your darkest moment, when you're frustrated, when you're uncertain, when you don't know what to do, you will have an online portal which will guide you each step of the way."*

Do you see how that sounds very different from a membership site? It addresses the hurts, the wants, the needs, and the desired outcome.

Then you'll overcome their objections by being specific. That way your right-fit prospect will be able to say to themselves, "this is for me" – while at the same time, you'll actually be repelling the people who your membership isn't right for.

Remember! My goal for you is to have the right-fit members, so that they will stay in your membership. Getting a wrong-fit member means they'll cancel.

This is why I want you to help them overcome objections by being specific. And guess what? In that specific statement, you're going to repel the wrong-fit members.

## Everyone's Favorite Channel

Next you need to make sure to answer the WIIFM – "What's In It For Me?"

One of my mentors, Dan Kennedy, said that every person is tuned into their own radio station called WIIFM. Everybody has their antenna up and it's tuned in to WIIFM. What's in it for me? When they read your email, or your sales page, they will be asking the question, "What's in it for me?"

Answer that question.

You'll do that through this painted picture you've been creating.

Now I want you to take this "picture" and hang it in your office. I want you to put it on your desk, have it there, and just continue to add to it.

You might find out as you have real-life conversations with your prospects and participate in different Facebook groups and on social media, "Oh, they're struggling with this. Let me write that down."

As you read articles and continue to learn more and more about your prospects, you'll also learn things about their wants, their pain points, their needs, and their desires. Write these things down and continue to build out this painted picture.

That's how you leverage this process.

It will enable you to communicate on a *much deeper level*. I'm not asking you to do this exercise so that you will have this nice little paragraph to put someplace.

No, I'm asking you to do this so that you can make sure you have a successful, fast launch for your membership... and so that you will be able to serve the people who really need you!

# 9 | THE LAUNCH STRATEGY THAT GUARANTEES YOU MEMBERS

You're probably saying to yourself, "I've been doing a lot of work on my right-fit members. But how do I know people will actually sign up for my membership?" After all, no one wants to start a membership and only get one or two signups.

I'm going to give you a strategy that will help you get your first members. It's a strategy that nobody else is teaching.

You might be familiar with the term "Founding Member," but I'm going to introduce you to a different concept that will *guarantee* you get members.

Does that sound like something you want? Do you want a guarantee that you'll get members?

That's what this chapter's all about.

Let me show you how to get your first members.

## Founding Members vs. *Launch Members*

There's always that question, "How do I know people will sign up?"

A lot of people teach the use of "Founding Members," but I'm going to teach you something new.

- **Founding Members** are the very first members you sell into your membership. You're probably familiar with this term and concept. They get the Founding Member rate, which they qualify for and receive as long as they don't cancel.

For example, let's say you put your Founding Membership offer out there at $997 – and those members get to lock in that $997 rate for as long as they don't cancel. It's a great way to get members using this strategy.

Your Founding Member offer works as a public promotion that gives people their first opportunity to join in the membership. They're willing to grow with your membership and understand that the membership site is still a work in progress and there may still be glitches. But because the deal's so good... they're willing to overlook those minor things and grow alongside you with your membership.

Your Founding Member is a really good member. You need Founding Members, and I absolutely recommend you do a launch focused on getting Founding Members.

But I want to introduce to you another strategy:

*Launch Members.*

There is a big difference between Launch Members and Founding Members. They are two entirely different types of members.

- **Launch Members** are seed members that you give FREE access to your coaching program.

You might ask, "Why would I do that?"

Well, I've seen a number of people go out and do a Founding Member launch, but only get 3-5 members. Honestly, that's a bit of a rough start because not all of them will show up for everything. And not all of them will become active in the community.

It's actually quite hard to get your membership off the ground with just 3-5 members.

If you instead use Launch Members, to whom you've given free access, these people will already be in the membership ahead of your Founding Member launch. They will be your welcoming committee that already know the ropes and are already there and active in your membership community.

When you do your Founding Member launch, you will have another group of members there who will act as a larger community to help you build your membership.

Your Launch Members will join by private invitation only – not a public launch or public promotion. It's a private invite that you give to a specific group of people. You invite them to become a Launch Member in your membership and give you honest feedback.

You will do this *before* you go out with your main public launch, and *before* you go out with your Founding Member launch. You will be able to use the feedback of these Launch Members to guide the design of the membership you offer for your Founding Members.

Then, you will take the feedback from your Founding Members and build upon that before you go public and go big with your membership launch.

## Why Launch Members Make Sense

Having taught this before, I know that some people will get hung up on the fact that you're gifting a membership to some initial Launch Members. "Why would you do that?"

We do that because we are asking for high-value feedback in exchange.

Remember, it doesn't have to be free forever. You can say something like, "Hey, can I give you a membership for the first four months? All I ask in return is for you to be willing to provide me some feedback."

Wouldn't you exchange a few free months in return for quality feedback and testimonials?

Wouldn't it be awesome to have testimonials *before* you try to get your Founding Members? It gives you real testimonials that demonstrate proof of concept for your membership.

That's what you're doing here with this Launch Membership.

You invite them to participate for just a limited time. It's not forever.

## Let Me Demonstrate This to You...

Years ago, my older brother used to manage some Arby's restaurants. He was opening up a brand-new restaurant and said, "Hey, listen, why don't you and your family come out and be part of our friends and family soft launch?"

"What's that?" I asked.

"We have our employees and their friends and family come out and eat at the restaurant for free."

"Why would you do that?"

"It lets us put our systems to the test. We're able to have our staff take the orders, then process the orders so the cooks in the back can make the food. It gives everybody an opportunity to test the systems."

"Okay."

"And by the way, you're going to get some free food."

"Hey, count us in!"

So, we went, and we were part of the friends and family soft launch. It was closed to the public – not open to anyone but us – and we were able to get some free food. And not only were we able to get some free food, but we were able to give some feedback.

During the event, my brother walked around, talking to people, asking things like:

- "How long did it take for you to place your order?"
- "How long did it take for you to receive your order?"
- "How hot was the food?"
- "Was there anything that you didn't like?"
- "Is there anything that we could do to improve the service?"

He asked these questions and got real feedback from people who had a genuine interest in the success of his restaurant.

*Businesses do this all the time.*

This isn't anything new. It is a proven concept that's used in multiple industries. They invite people in and give them free access in exchange for valuable feedback.

This is what I want you to provide for your launch members: free access and an opportunity for you to get feedback, so you can make sure your systems work, make sure your coaching program works, make sure your membership site works, and get valuable feedback before you even do your Founding Member launch.

Listen, I know Founding Members can be forgiving at times, and they're going to overlook some errors. But what they won't overlook is consistent errors. That's what you will be able to avoid by having Launch Members test your process and offering first.

These are people who genuinely want you to succeed. They can be your friends. They can be your family. They can even be people who are *not* your right-fit members. That's okay. They just want to see you succeed, so why not use them? Why not gift it to them and allow them to see the inside of your membership?

Who knows? You might actually learn more from them than you would from your Founding Members.

## Here's What I Want You to Do...

It's a little bit of a workshop...

Name 10 people you can invite to become Launch Members.

The reason I have you name 10 is because there's a chance that not all of them will say yes. Maybe they will just think about it. But even if only 5 out of 10 people do this, think about the community they can provide for your Founding Members. Think about the excitement they're going to help generate!

Because you'll say to them, "Hey listen, part of this is I want you to celebrate other members as they join. I want you to welcome them. I want you to chat them up in the private Facebook group." (If that's what you do.)

You're creating a foundation of people who want you to succeed and are going to be there for you so that you won't have to do this alone.

Right now, name 10 people who are going to be your Launch Members. Write them down in your notes.

Now... *invite them in!*

# Part 3

# Scale Your Sales Without Selling

# 10 | PRICING STRATEGIES TO HELP YOU LAUNCH

"How should I price my high-ticket coaching program?"

"What if I don't want to start with a high-ticket offer?"

These are common questions. Everybody wants to know the "right" answer, and fears getting it wrong, causing people to not sign up because of the price of membership.

This chapter will help you overcome those fears by showing you a couple of pricing models to help you make the decision of how to price your membership.

I need to say up front that this is something I can't decide for you. There are a lot of factors involved with pricing your membership. For example, you might have fixed costs involved with your membership, or costs related to delivery of physical goods or there may even be costs associated with meetings and events.

We'll talk about how to handle all that.

Or you might run your membership purely digitally, where everything is delivered online with minimal fixed costs.

We'll talk about that as well.

But that's only the beginning of the factors involved when it comes to choosing the right price for your coaching program. To walk you through this process and help you make the decision, let's look at some different strategies.

## The Impact Pricing Strategy

The first strategy I want to share with you is called the *Impact Pricing Strategy*. This is where you price your membership at a low cost so you can impact more people.

Pricing your membership at a very low investment is done with the intent to get as many people as possible to sign up for your coaching program. This strategy focuses on maximizing the breadth, not the depth, of your membership.

By creating a low barrier to entry, the Impact Pricing Strategy allows you to serve as many people as possible.

This might *not* be the right strategy for everyone.

It's really best for those wanting to put out a message to a broad audience, and possibly use it as a way to later up-level members into a high-ticket membership offer.

The goal is often mission driven for coaches in this situation. Having a low price assists you to expand your mission.

When I was President of Church Leader Insights, we had a coaching program called "The Renegade Pastor." Our goal was to help pastors "abandon average." That was our mission. We were dedicated to doing everything possible to come alongside pastors and encourage them in their ministry.

In order to accomplish that mission, we priced the coaching program at $99 per month. We knew that we would be able to reach as many pastors as possible and create a sustainable coaching program with that investment.

Currently, I have a group called Membership Accelerators Club. The goal with this group is to help as many membership and coaching businesses serve their members as possible.

I get to lay my head down at night knowing that I'm vicariously helping numerous people develop better relationships, better marriages, experience financial freedom, get healthy and so much more. All because members of the Membership Accelerators Club are out there getting and serving more members.

I price this membership low enough to attract more people so that I can have a broader impact. (But I also have a high-ticket offer.)

## The Outcome Pricing Strategy

The *Outcome Pricing Strategy* is where you price your membership with a high-ticket offer so that you can create a greater outcome for a smaller number of people.

The idea is that by setting a higher barrier to entry, you can still generate greater income so that you can offer a higher level of service to fewer people.

By the way, this is where I have chosen to price my high-ticket membership offer. I have chosen to work with a smaller number of people so that I can create a greater outcome for them. Currently, my high-ticket membership offer is $5,000 per month. Yes, per month!

This would be the strategy you'd want to consider if you desire to work more deeply with fewer people. Your main concern isn't necessarily the mission, but it's more about the outcome you can deliver for your members. I want to know that I'm able to deliver the outcome for my members and so I price it high, recognizing that I'm going to get fewer people, but those people may be more serious about implementation.

Consider this for a moment...

I could have chosen to go for the impact and just price it as low as possible to attract a large number of people. But I really wanted to know that I was getting the right people, those who weren't just going to *subscribe* to the membership. I wanted to get people who were going to be serious about *implementation*. Therefore, I can know I will have a greater outcome with an individual, as opposed to a broader gathering of people.

Members of my high-ticket coaching program consistently add six or seven figures per year to their business as a direct result of working with me. It's not uncommon for some of them to double their business in a year.

The harsh truth is, they would not have hired me if I didn't charge $5,000 per month. No joke! I've asked.

One of my long-time members, Mike Agugliaro, said to me, "If you priced your coaching program lower, I would have never hired you. I wouldn't have thought the investment was worth it or worth my time."

You have to choose the Outcome Pricing Strategy or the Impact Pricing Strategy. Those really are the two different pricing models.

When it comes to pricing your membership you need to decide:

- Are you going for *breadth* (maximizing impact)?
- Or are you going for *depth* (maximizing outcome)?

## Other Factors to Consider...

When you choose your regular membership rate, you want to select an amount you can adjust downward to create an appropriate and compelling Founding Member rate.

For example, you probably wouldn't want to choose a $497 membership without taking into consideration what your Founding Member rate will be.

It's important to consider both – because remember, you'll want to do a Founding Member launch.

Then beyond that, I want you to also know what your future membership rate could be.

For instance, when we've launched memberships, we've always planned for a regular rate (such as $1500) and then a Founding Member rate (such as $997). But we would always be able to say that eventually this membership may cost $1500, $2000, or even $2500 per month.

That way you're able to price against what the future rate could potentially become. I want you to be able to say something like: "The Founding Member rate is $997 and after that goes away, it's going to be $1500. And eventually, my membership may be $2000, or $2500."

Important Note: I am *not* saying to price your high-ticket membership at $1500 and your Founding Member rate at $997. This is for illustrative use only and has been utilized by my clients.

What I *am* saying is I want you to choose your regular rate first, and then create your Founding Member rate based off that, along with what you want the future rate to become if all goes well and you continue to grow your membership.

Price your membership today at your regular rate, your Founding Member rate, and then – say 2-3 years from now – what you think those future rates should be.

Let me give you a bad example. Let's say the regular rate is $1500 and the Founding Member rate is $1400. And then, it's decided that the future rates could be $1600, $1700, or $1800.

You might ask, "Why is that a bad example?"

First, it goes against the principle of making sure your Founding Member discounted rate is significantly less than your regular rate. By dropping the price only $100, that difference is not a motivating factor. There has to be a *significant* difference between the two price points.

Make sure your Founding Member rate is significantly less than your regular rate. And then make sure your future rates are considerably more.

## Don't Talk Yourself Out of Selling a High-Ticket Offer

I know where your mind is going to go... you're going to talk yourself out of pricing your membership offer where potentially you think it should be.

Let's say you have one member investing $1000 a month or you have 10 members investing $100 a month.

It's the same amount of revenue – $1000.

I want you to understand something important:

> *It's NOT TEN times harder to sell ONE member at $1000 a month than it is to sell TEN members at $100 a month.*

If anything, it's potentially more difficult to get 10 members at $100 dollars a month than just going after the one member at $1000 a month.

Why am I sharing this with you?

Because you're going to have this myth swirling around in your mind that if you price your membership at that higher price point, it's going to make it harder to sell.

That is not always true.

What makes it harder for you to sell is *trying to sell to the wrong people.*

That one member who's willing to invest at $1000 a month is a different person than the 10 people at $100 a month. These are two totally different audiences, totally different people, totally different wallets.

It's absolutely not 10 times harder, *as long as you're selling to the right people.*

Consider, "Who is my audience and what are they willing to invest?" Let me give you some questions to help guide you.

## DOES THE PRICE ATTRACT MY IDEAL MEMBER?

Remember when I said earlier that the one person willing to invest $1000 is a different type of person than the 10 people at $100?

You want to attract your ideal member – and if your ideal member is someone who is willing to invest $100, then go and price it accordingly.

But if your ideal member is willing to invest $1000 a month, why would you price it at $100?

To attract your ideal member with your pricing, you need to know they're able to invest that amount.

## DOES THE PRICE REFLECT THE FINANCIAL OUTCOME OF THE MEMBERSHIP?

You may have promised some kind of financial outcome that results from joining your membership. For example, my membership promises: "I will help you get more members and help you multiply your recurring revenue."

I want my members to know that the investment they make in my membership reflects a financial model of a 10x investment. If they invest $100 in one of my membership programs, we're able to generate $1000 for them.

For somebody who invests $10,000 in one of my VIP days, I want them to know they're able to generate multiple six figures as a result – and I've been able to meet this outcome every single time. (In fact, Mike Agugliaro generated a *million dollars* in 21 days, just from our VIP Day together. It makes me want to price my VIP Day a little bit higher when I see that number!)

Therefore, if your membership is providing some sort of financial outcome or return on investment, does your pricing reflect that?

I'm not saying it has to be 10 times the investment. Sometimes it could be 3 times. Sometimes it could be 5 times. Sometimes it could be 20 times.

I just want *my* members to know that I'm consistently able to provide at least 10 times return on investment. (Again, some months it may be lower, some months it may be higher, but at a bare minimum, I want them to know that.)

## DOES THE PRICE REFLECT THE PROMISED OUTCOME OF THE MEMBERSHIP?

If your membership doesn't offer a financial outcome, this question is for you.

Maybe you're in the health and fitness space, where you're helping people get healthy, then helping them stay fit. Or maybe you help people with their marriage, their parenting skills, whatever it may be.

Does the price reflect the promised outcome of the membership?

- Does it help them save time?
- Does it help them avoid stress?
- Does it help them to have better relationships?

And if so, does that investment cost reflect that same level of outcome?

For example, if I said to you that I can help you have a healthy marriage for just $7 a month, does that really sound right?

I mean, if I say to prospects: "My wife and I just celebrated 25 years of marriage and we've learned how to build happy, healthy, and sustainable relationships. That's why I could help people have a healthy marriage for just $7," ... does that make sense? *No!*

You want your pricing to reflect the impact the promised outcome will provide. Somebody who's going to go to marriage counseling can invest $150 to $200 per session.

You want to know that your membership is going to deliver what it promises and that it is going to be a worthwhile investment – where the price accurately reflects the promised outcome of the membership.

## ARE THERE HARD COSTS INVOLVED WITH THE MEMBERSHIP?

As a business coach, you most likely have very few hard costs. You might have an office space that you rent or maybe one day you desire to have a space where you can hold events for your members.

Hard costs to factor into your pricing:

- You need to pay yourself first. What's your time worth?

- Costs of employees

- Costs of deliverables, such as physical products, event meeting space, etc.

You may need to do a bit more planning if you have deliverables. For instance, what if the price of goods goes up? What if shipping costs escalate? If that happens, are you going to be able to maintain the margins on your membership?

If you know that you have hard costs like a physical product involved, then I want you to take that into consideration when pricing.

Many high-ticket memberships often include events. Will you be able to cover meeting space, meals, travel, and other related costs with the way your membership is priced?

Plus, over time, you will want to pay yourself more. You're going to want to make more money. Don't get caught in the trap of always having to attract more members in order to get paid more. You can get paid more by controlling costs and increasing your retention (but that's a subject for a different book).

Be sure to factor all these elements into your margin when you price your membership. I don't want you to ever get in a position where the hard costs of your membership have risen so much that now your membership is no longer profitable.

## HOW DOES MY PRICE COMPARE TO OTHERS?

You may see people who are in your same niche who are already serving your audience. What are they charging? What is your audience currently investing in those other memberships?

You might also consider what these same individuals are willing to invest in other memberships or other products and services outside of your niche. If somebody's willing to invest $997 a month in a membership that has nothing to do with your niche, maybe they'd be willing to invest $997 a month with you.

## DOES THE PRICE ENABLE ME TO INCREASE IT LATER?

I want you to be able to price your membership in such a way that you have future pricing in mind.

I want you to be able to say to yourself, "Hey, this membership could potentially go up to $1500, $2000, $2500..."

Have that future pricing in mind when you establish your current pricing.

To wrap up, make sure to ask yourself all these questions:

- What is my regular rate?
- What is my Founding Member rate?
- What will be the future rate for my membership?

Don't buy into the myth that it's going to be harder to sell your membership just because you priced it higher. No, it's actually going to be easier to sell... as long as you have the right audience, which we talked about earlier to pinpoint your right-fit member.

Nail this down and then let's continue to a really important topic – how to scale your membership without selling.

# 11 | ENTICING PEOPLE TO JOIN NOW

Everybody wants to think that the Founding Member rate is going to be what motivates people the most to sign up *right now*. That's not always the case.

Price doesn't always make the difference for people to take action. There are other ways you can entice them to join your membership beyond just a Founding Member rate.

## Offer Fast Action Bonuses

One of the ways to entice people to join now is to use *Fast Action Bonuses*. When you first start out, this is a good tactic to both sell your membership and get people to sign up and act immediately.

Even when you have a special offer for your existing membership, always include bonuses. It's just a matter of layering on reasons why people should take action.

Note that if you have products or resources, you can use those as a fast action bonus.

For example, for my low-ticket membership I offer those who buy my book to take a "free test drive of the Membership Accelerators Club as a Fast Action Bonus."

Or I could make the offer: "Everybody who joins the Membership Accelerators Club gets a copy of my book, and receives over $900 in bonus resources and trainings."

When someone joins my high-ticket membership, they get access to *all* my trainings. They get access to my events and more importantly they get access to me.

Look over your membership for items that you could pull out to make available as fast action bonuses.

## ALWAYS PROVIDE A DOLLAR VALUE

Make sure to provide the value of your bonuses as a real money amount. For example, when you promote your membership say, "The Founding Member rate is going to be just $997 as opposed to the regular rate of $1500," so people can make that price comparison easily.

But if I say, "You're also going to get this free bonus," it doesn't mean as much. Sure, the bonus is for free, but what is it *worth?*

Instead say, "You get this free bonus valued at $2000 when you join." That makes people want to take action. They'll say, "Oh, I get a $2000 bonus just by signing up now."

Provide the dollar value for your bonuses.

## FAST IMPLEMENTATION CALL

Another way to entice people to join is to give them a Fast Implementation Call.

In the past I've offered: "You're going to get a membership maximizer zoom call, one-on-one with me, valued at $497."

That $497 is a real value. If one of my clients calls me up and says, "Hey, I need one of those maximizer zoom calls," they know the investment for a one-hour zoom call is $497. But someone who signs up from the offer will get it for free, and that gives them a substantial feeling of confidence and allows them to more easily make the decision to sign up now.

## OUTRAGEOUS GIFT

Another bonus idea would be an Outrageous Gift.

I've used this style offer: "Get my social media advertising swipe file as an outrageous gift... and not only mine, but my private clients as well."

I've been able to share my private clients' Facebook ads along with my own Facebook ads and put them together in a collection to create a social media swipe file that I can provide as a gift.

This Outrageous Gift has a legitimate $5,000 value.

By the way, if you would like to receive this "Most Outrageous Gift" just go to www.FastLaunchCoach.com and get your free resources.

## SWIPE FILES

As evidenced above, a collection of tools that work can be very enticing as an Outrageous Gift, or simply frame it as a Swipe File.

I used the same principle when I offered this bonus:

> "The Million Dollar Membership Sales Page and Swipe File – you're going to get my swipe file that's literally responsible for over $7 million in membership sales, a legitimate $5,000 value."

Again, it's just a swipe file that people were able to take and use for themselves.

## Apply the Scarcity Principle

What do I mean by the *Scarcity Principle*? The Scarcity Principle means only the next X-number-of-people who sign up will be able to get in on this opportunity.

For example, you can say your Founding Member rate is $997 but *only the first 10 people who sign up* will get that rate. There's a limited number of spots available.

Later, after you've started the promotion, you can message people that there are only 5 spots left or only 4 spots left or only 3.

You could also apply the scarcity principle with your bonuses, such as only allowing the next 10 people who sign up to get your bonuses.

I do want to impress upon you the need for you to be a person of integrity whenever you apply scarcity. I really want you to honor what you say you're going to do. If you're opening 10 spots, and only the next 10 spots are going to get these bonuses, then I want you to honor that.

You might say, "Well Scott, what if that 11th person comes in and asks to sign up and get the bonuses?"

In that kind of case, I like to say:

> "Hey, my apologies, but it looks like you're the 11th person. Unfortunately, somebody always has to be the 11th person. Here's what I want you to know. I'm a person of integrity. And I know that you would not want me to violate my integrity to honor those bonuses to you and not be truthful to everyone else in my audience. So instead, here's what I would like to do. I can't give you all those bonuses I mentioned there, but I could give you some of those bonuses. And I could throw in this gift over here as well. Now, again, I don't want to violate my integrity. But what I'd like to do is create another special opportunity just for you. Okay?"

What I'm doing here is demonstrating my integrity.

I want you to also be a person of integrity. Your prospects will honor that.

That's why I included the line, "I know you would not want me to violate my integrity to the rest of my audience." That *is* what people are doing indirectly, though. When they come in after the offer has run out, yet ask you to waive the limit, they're actually putting you in that spot of violating your integrity.

I always turn it around and say, "Hey, I know you're not asking me to violate my integrity. Here's what I would like to do instead..."

That's very important. People respect and honor those who do what they say. And this will make them like you even more, because you're not just trying some marketing gimmick or trick, but you're actually acting as a person of integrity.

Afterward they say to themselves, "It looks like I lost out, but I appreciate the willingness to give me a different opportunity and a different sign-up bonus in response."

Therefore, use these tactics, but I want you to utilize them with integrity.

## Create Urgency with a Deadline

Having said that about scarcity, let's also talk about creating urgency with a deadline.

With a deadline on your membership, you let your prospects know that the opportunity to get these bonuses for the next X-number-of-people ends on a specific date and time.

What I'm *not* saying is this means you close your enrollment period. I don't want you to close your membership offering at that time; I want people to be able to sign up *all the time.* But when you offer bonuses as an incentive to act now, utilize scarcity by adding a deadline so that this offer – this special opportunity – goes away.

Here is an example for you. On the thank you page that appears after registering for a webinar, you could run a video congratulating the prospect on having registered for the webinar and to look for a confirmation email that will arrive in a moment.

"In the meantime, here's a special one-time opportunity for you that disappears in X minutes..."

Then below the video, you show them a countdown timer, already practically to the end of that countdown timer, quickly ticking away.

You might be thinking, "Well, Scott. But how can I do this?" Even if the technology for this is a bit more advanced than you can feel comfortable, don't skip the principle. Instead, you can just say in that video, "This opportunity ends Friday at midnight" and when it's Friday at midnight, then the special is over.

I did something like this before with a special offer we promoted. And I even said in my email, "Hey, don't contact me on Saturday saying you missed it. I'm a person of integrity. This opportunity is going to go away."

Well, I guess somebody didn't believe me. They emailed me on Saturday and said, "Hey, your sales page is missing."

I thought to myself, "It's actually because it's after the deadline and they missed out."

Things like that will happen. But maintain your integrity. Once people see that you follow through on what you say you will do, they will be even more inclined to trust your word in the future.

Plus, someone who will eagerly push your ethical boundaries for personal gain is never going to be a right-fit member!

## Leverage Your Guarantee

Yes, you really can have a guarantee on your membership.

My guarantee goes like this:

*"Hey, if you sign up for the membership and decide that it's not right for you, that it's not a good fit, then let me know and I'll refund your investment within the first 30 days."*

I'm not going to refund their investment if they signed up six months ago and finally decided they don't like the membership and they want their money back for the entire six months.

No. I'll give a refund within the first 30 days.

If somebody says to me, "I want to cancel my membership this month," and they were charged for the first time yesterday, I'll refund them. After all, they were only charged yesterday.

You make those judgment calls in the best interests of your member.

Another guarantee idea:

*"We drink our own Kool-Aid. We want to give you every opportunity to put the sales system into action and experience the joy you feel when you wake up each morning to find new leads opting into your list. So instead of a traditional 30-day guarantee, you have two full months to go through the program and follow the plan. Use the bonuses and get your system up and running. If after a full 60 days, if you've done*

*all the work but still have nothing to show for it, you're entitled to your money back."*

## Use These Strategies to Drive Signups

Here are the four ways I have shared with you to entice people to sign up:

- Offer fast action bonuses
- Apply scarcity
- Create urgency with the deadline
- Leverage your guarantee

Though you don't have to use all of these, I think you definitely should use fast action bonuses and always have a deadline if you're going to make an offer. You could just use those two.

Or you could apply scarcity and say, "The next 10 people who sign up are going to get this rate (or these bonuses), but it ends on the deadline. And by the way, you can cancel at any time and you have 30 days to test it out. Within the first 30 days, you can decide, and if this membership isn't right for you, I'll refund your investment."

Leverage these to entice people to sign up for your membership right now.

Next, let's talk about how to scale yourself without selling...

# 12 | YOUR FIRST (AND NEXT) MEMBERSHIP SITE

You may be asking: "What about my membership site? How do I even set something like that up?"

Many people believe that to launch their membership, they need to have a membership site set up first. That's not true.

As a matter of fact, one of my clients is soon launching a new membership – and the membership site itself isn't going to be ready for another three weeks. But she's already selling people into the program.

You don't have to have everything in line before you make it happen. Don't let the tech get in the way. All too often people get stuck and let technology barriers prohibit them from actually starting their membership.

Consider this. I launched a membership back in 2009, back when Facebook was just getting started and before there were Facebook groups, Facebook ads, or any of that. There wasn't even such a thing as a membership site. I mean, it just didn't exist.

If I was able to launch a membership before membership sites and Facebook groups existed, then you can do it as well.

You might be saying, "Well Scott, times are different. We *do* have Facebook groups. We *do* have membership sites. People kind of expect that."

Not always. They may expect it to happen at some point, but it doesn't have to be immediately.

Let's make a commitment to start simple. Don't get stuck in the tech. Don't think you have to have everything all together. Just make it *very simple*. I know some who have delivered their membership content via email, with only links in the email to a training video or resource or bonuses. With just little links sent via email, they have provided significant value to their members.

Start simple. Allow your membership site to grow with your membership. People don't necessarily expect everything to already be in place.

## Imagine You're Starting a Restaurant...

In some respects, we're talking about starting a business.

Let's say you had decided to open a restaurant from scratch. You'd probably be thinking something like this:

- 15,000-square-foot building
- Two kitchens
- Dining room and a separate bar area
- And it's going to be the best restaurant you've ever seen!

That's a big risk, especially for someone starting from scratch who has never run a restaurant before.

Do you really think getting a 15,000-square-foot building for your restaurant is the best thing to do right now? What if people don't like the food? What if they don't like the ambiance?

Wouldn't it be wise to instead start out with a proof of concept first? Maybe get a 3000-square-foot building and start your restaurant small, build up your customer base...

Make sure that people like the food, like the ambience, like the environment...

And *then* grow from there into a larger building... and then a larger building... until finally, you've got that 15,000-square-foot building from your dreams.

That's the right way to approach this as well. Allow your membership to grow with you and with your members.

I mean, what a joy it would be for your members to receive a communication from you saying, "Hey, we're always looking to improve the ways we serve our members. And because of our growth, we're making updates to our membership site, and we've got some great things planned, so be on the lookout!"

Then when you do this big unveiling of your new membership site – leaving behind the one that got you started – you can replace it with one you can grow into even further.

Remember: allow your membership site to grow with your membership.

## Don't Try to Build a Ferrari on a Volkswagen Budget

So many people want to build amazing membership sites. They want badges, they want to track people's progress, they want to send out rewards. They want to do all of this and more.

They're trying to build a Ferrari, but they've only got a Volkswagen budget.

Listen, you're just starting... go with the Volkswagen first.

We all had our first car, right? Mine was a 1989 Ford Tempo. They don't even make Ford Tempos anymore. Now I drive a BMW Z4. I wasn't a kid driving a BMW Z4, and I definitely did not have that caliber of a membership site with my first membership offer either.

Start out small, build with it, and allow it to grow.

Remember, it is possible to sell your membership without having your membership site built yet. You see, having members signing up is a great motivating factor to get your tech set up. Why not have your members pay you to build out your membership site?

"Wait a second," you say. "You mean people will actually join my membership and pay up front and I can utilize that money to get my membership site built?"

Yes.

Why not do it that way?

You just have to fulfill what you promised you were going to deliver. Why not allow new members to pay you to build your membership site? Just get one built and grow from there.

That's the goal. I really do believe that some people use the challenge of building out their membership site as a reason or excuse to *not* grow, to *not* focus on getting members, and to *not* focus on helping people. Don't let that be you.

## Choose a Technology for Your Site and Grow with It

Let me give you a few technology options you can use to get your membership site started.

You could go for a totally free membership site and use a Facebook group or a WordPress page.

You might be thinking, "Well, I need a secure login for my WordPress membership site pages, so my stuff won't get given out free to the whole world."

Honestly, just set up a page and don't worry about securing it.

I mean, we're talking about your Founding Members here. Are they really going to go and broadcast their login information to the world?

Don't worry about having a login page for now either. Just set up a website where members can go. That's where you will put your membership resources.

Or you could store them in a Facebook group. (If you don't know what I mean by Facebook groups, just Google it – but you can put videos in there, attachments, PDFs, all sorts of stuff. You can also create Facebook lives there, which are live video sessions your members can attend or watch later. Plus, it's free. Just use one of these options to get started.

The client I mentioned earlier launched her membership by sending everybody to a Facebook group. Note that this is a multimillion-dollar membership, and she's sending people to a free Facebook group.

She has multiple staff members, yet she's still utilizing a free option. She even has full-time tech people who could build out a membership site, but instead she chose to focus on serving and getting people into her membership.

There are also low-cost membership sites like Kajabi, Click Funnels, and CustomerHub, among others.

Do this...

*Just choose one and go.*

My philosophy on membership sites is like choosing a CRM (customer relationship management software that helps you manage email lists and client data)... just choose the best of the worst. They all have their pluses and minuses. They all have features that are different from one another. And they all come at different price levels.

Just choose one. You can always change it later.

Don't assume that because you're choosing one now, you have to stick with it forever. You can definitely swap it later after you have members. For now, just choose one that's going to best suit your needs today.

For example, if you use video, make sure the service is able to host video for you. If you need unlimited downloads, make sure it offers that. Whatever. Choose one to get you started and allow people to pay you to build out your membership site while you grow.

If you want a customizable membership site, there are a couple of options.

For my site, we use Keap (formerly InfusionSoft) and we use WordPress. I invested a great deal of money in hiring a developer to build out my platform, and I used WordPress so I could control things and it would be customizable. But when I first started this business, I just used one of those free deals.

Go out and create a free Facebook group and then have people start paying you for your membership program. Then move on to a low-cost membership site after you've done the free. And then after you grow some more, grow into something that's customizable.

Let me give you a final caution...

## Don't Get Fancy with Your Site

Please don't think you've got to have this plugin or that plugin before you can get rolling. Before you know it, you would be spending all your money on those different plugins that your members won't care about.

They truly care less about your membership site and more about what you promise with your membership.

Let that one sink in for a moment.

*Your members could not care less about the technology behind your membership site.*

The only people who talk about membership sites are people who run memberships. I never hear members saying, "Wow, I wish they used Kajabi instead of ClickFunnels." I don't even hear members saying, "Wow, I wish they used Kajabi instead of a free Facebook group."

No. The only people who talk about membership sites are the ones who run memberships or people who sell the software.

Instead, care about what your members care about – the outcome and the promise of what you said you were going to deliver. Care about that.

I've seen multimillion-dollar memberships run on some of the most basic platforms, where literally millions of dollars have been made... and their membership is being handled by software that costs $50 per month.

There are so many people in this business out there just trying to make ends meet – making $1,000-2,000 a month in recurring revenue – with a membership site that's costing them $500 a month.

Why would they do that? I've never had a member cancel because our membership site didn't have some sort of plugin. I never had a member complain because we didn't give badges or track completion on courses. I've never had a member cancel because of something like that.

No. The only people who care about those things are the ones trying to sell you the software. Don't focus on it. Your goal is to launch and launch fast. If you're not tech savvy, choose something free and easy and grow from there.

## No Tech Gets in the Way

That's my mantra. *No tech gets in the way.*

How do you do that?

There are some websites I recommend where you can outsource and have someone else make the technology work for you.

For example, let's say you don't know how to set up Kajabi or ClickFunnels. Guess what? You can hire somebody. Go to UpWork.com. You can interview, hire, and let someone else do it for you.

I use this service. I'll send some tasks for ClickFunnels, pay around $50, and the person will set up an entire funnel for me. For just $50.

You know how long it would take me to set that up? Hours. Meanwhile, that person can get it done in no time.

You can also use Fiverr.com. Just be careful as sometimes they have a lower range of skill set for membership sites. But for graphics, definitely use Fiverr to outsource the daunting tech.

You could also go to Facebook and join their Kajabi group or ClickFunnels group. Post your question inside that Facebook group, asking, "Hey, how do I make this work?" I've seen people respond with videos saying, "I just recorded this video tutorial for you. Here's how to do it."

People actually have questions answered right inside those Facebook user groups! Search for Infusionsoft or Keap or

ClickFunnels or Kajabi or whatever. They all have their own Facebook groups.

Another site is www.onlinejobs.ph. Why is that .ph? Well, it's the Philippines. We've hired people from onlinejobs.ph and I could get a full-time employee for just a couple hundred dollars for an entire month. I'm not kidding. The exchange rate here from the U.S. to the Philippines is substantial. A couple hundred dollars provides them a really good lifestyle.

Make sure the person you choose has credibility. Check their other work and references, but then let them do the work for you.

Don't assume the tech is going to be so big and so outrageous that you can't do it yourself. But you probably shouldn't be doing it. Instead, you should stay focused on getting members and delivering value to your membership. Let somebody else take care of the tech for you. Just make a decision, stick with it, and grow. And then as you grow, develop your next membership site.

That's why I called this chapter "your first (and next) membership site." It never stops. You just continue to improve.

# 13 | CREATING YOUR SALES LETTER

Let's talk about creating your sales letter to invite people to join your membership.

And that's the thing I really wanted you to understand – you're *inviting* people into membership. It's not some sort of hard sell or anything like that. Instead, it really is an invitation to join.

I'm going to walk you through the process for creating that sales letter, but before we deep dive into that, you need to identify answers to a few important questions. When we write your sales letter, you have to know your target.

Go back to that ideal prospective member description we created earlier and pull it out. (Remember I told you to write everything down?) Here's where you start looking at who your ideal prospect is, so we can determine how you're going to reach them, and then write your sales letter to that target.

## Questions to Ask Before You Write Your Letter

Begin to answer these questions now because they're going to come into your sales letter.

- **What keeps your ideal member awake at night?** You've got a membership that's going to deliver on an outcome to solve this... so what makes them lose sleep at night? What are they afraid of? What are their fears?

- **What or who are they angry at?** Do they feel like there's a system against them? Do they feel like there are people working against them and against their success? Who or what are they angry at?

- **What are their top three daily frustrations?** What causes them stress as they go about their day, as they lay down to sleep at night? What's going on in their life that frustrates them daily?

- **What trends are occurring in their business or life?** Think about the trends they may be facing and dealing with today. Let's use the health and fitness niche because it's an easy example that we probably all relate to. There are diet trends everyone in that marketplace has to address. For example, keto had a big trend. What are the trends going on now in your niche?

- **What does your ideal member secretly desire most?** I mean, do they desire more money, more freedom, more respect? What is it?

- **Are you selling to the person who's able to make the decision?** It could be that someone – a boss, a spouse, a board of directors – is a built-in obstacle to your ideal prospect being able to make the decision to join your membership. It could be they report to somebody else and so they have a hurdle to overcome in order to take action.

- **Do they have their own language, their own vernacular?** I've had clients in the IT field, and others who were lawyers. I've also had clients who are in the service business. They all have their own language. You have to learn your right-fit member's language so you can use it inside your letter.

- **Who else is selling something similar to your membership?** If something already exists, go look at their sales page and examine what they wrote. However, do not ever assume that other people's sales pages are converting into *actual* sales, but just look at what theirs says and how they use language.

- **Who else has tried selling to your right-fit member but has failed?** In my world, there are people who've tried to sell membership marketing and membership success tools to others and have failed. I looked at what they did and what they said. Do the same in your market. See who else has tried selling to your ideal member but has failed, then look at what they did and what they said.

Now that you've answered those questions, it's time to dive into how to craft an effective sales letter.

## The Elements of an Effective Sales Letter

I'm now going to provide you with a complete sales letter template. Because it is a template, you can fill in the blanks with information specific to your audience and your membership. It's basically a swipe file that you can use to create your own sales letter.

I'm going to walk you through each of the different elements in this template, how to use them, and why they're important.

### 1. THE EYEBROW TEXT

The very first element is the eyebrow text. What is that? And why is it important? Here's an example from the template.

*Attention [insert target audience]:*
*Stop Putting Up With [Annoying Task or Problem] Forever!!!*

Right from the beginning, you want to call out your audience and your ideal prospective member. It could also be:

*Attention: Business Coaches Who Are
Tired of Struggling to Create
and Sell a High-Ticket Coaching Offer!*

Call out your audience in the eyebrow text.

2. THE HEADLINE

Then there's the headline.

**"Discover How You Can
Quickly And Easily
Get *[Big Benefit]* Guaranteed
To *[Insert Outcome They Want]*
Without *[Insert Annoying Problem]*!"**

You want to show them the benefit they desire – quickly and easily. You don't have to use the word guaranteed, but it's a powerful word if you can do so.

For example:

**"Discover How You Can
Quickly And Easily
Create and Sell a High-Ticket Offer
in the Next 30 Days Without Sounding Salesy!"**

This would be a headline for almost any marketplace of coaches.

3.THE SUB-HEADLINE.

The sub-headline is in a smaller font, right underneath the headline.

**And the most extraordinary thing about
this simple-to-use *[insert noun]* is how quickly it works.
You can *[insert outcome]* (or even more)
within just *[insert length of time]*!**

The sub-headline reinforces the headline. For example:

**And the most extraordinary thing about
this simple-to-use system is how quickly it works.
You can launch your high-ticket offer within just 30 days
(without the techy or expensive membership site)!**

## 4. GREETING

Then you have the greeting. The greeting is where you say, "Dear so-and-so."

> Dear Frustrated *[Insert target audience name]*,

You don't want to say, "Dear reader," you want to say, "Dear Frustrated Business Coach."

I want you to call out your target audience. If you're targeting business owners, don't say, "Dear General Business Owner," instead be specific... as in "Dear Frustrated Service Business Owner," or "Dear Frustrated Lawyer," or "Dear Frustrated Doctor."

## 5. YOUR LETTER

Next you begin the body of your letter. The letter has a number of different elements in it. You want to lead with:

> If you've ever wanted to *[insert benefit]* without hassling with the *[insert problem]* then this will be the most important message you'll ever read.
>
> Because I am going to show you how to *[insert outcome they want]* that'll allow you to *[insert benefit]*, you'll be able to *[insert outcome they want]* without having to deal with *[common problems your customers face when trying to solve this problem]*.

When you insert the benefit, note that the benefit is *not* to have a membership site. That's the actual modality by which you deliver the benefit. For example:

> If you ever wanted to impact more people without having to wonder when the next member will sign up, then this will be the most important message you'll ever read.

Because I'm going to show you how you can create a high-ticket coaching offer that'll position you to sell six or even seven figures of your business coaching. You'll be able to...

And from there you just continue on with the letter and start talking about your story and how you got started in membership.

First, tell people the most emotional rendition of the problem you're trying to solve. Then tell the story of how you managed to overcome all the stress, frustration, anxiety, or whatever, that led you to create your membership.

But before I do that, let me tell you a story of how I was able to overcome *[insert annoying problem]*...

[Here is where you tell the most emotional rendition of the problem you are trying to solve or the "desire" you are trying to fulfill. You want to make sure the story is no more than 250 words or so. Any longer and you'll start to talk about yourself more... and your sales letter MUST talk to the customer! If this isn't a personal story, you can use a case study of someone else who's gone through the same thing. But you MUST have a story!! People love stories and you'll get immediate attention if you have one!]

And then after experiencing that problem, that frustration, that pain, you decided to do something about it. Continue to fill in the letter by filling in the blanks provided in the template.

Talk about how your life changed forever after you made that discovery and took action.

### After Experiencing *[Insert Problem]* I Decided To Do Something About It!!!

[Here is where you talk about how your life was better when the problem was solved. Really lay on the benefits here. Don't introduce the Coaching Program yet... you're just hitting the prospect with benefits and getting them to imagine what it would be like to have the problem solved.]

So after I was able to *[overcome problem and get a solution]* I decided...

### Why Not Make The Ability To
### *[Solve Problem]* Available To Everyone!!!

So I decided to combine all the research... all the hours I spent researching *[insert problem]* into a single solution that'll make *[insert problem they're trying to solve]* a piece of cake.

You'll get all the tips and techniques that'll allow you to *[insert problem they're trying to solve]* when you invest in:

Of course, you're going to describe the solution you've discovered, which is your membership program.

# *[Name Of Coaching Program]*

*[Name of Coaching Program]* will enable anyone to *[insert problem they're trying to solve]* without having to *[insert common problems people face when working with said problem]*.

You'll get *[insert what they get... include number of meetings, subject matter of content, describe the community they'll join, etc. Insert as much detail as possible since your prospect cannot see your Coaching Program!]*. All of this was created from *[insert length of time, amount of effort it took to create the Coaching Program. This boosts value of your Coaching Program!]*.

You see, I am very proud of *[Coaching Program]*. Because after you join *[Coaching Program]* you'll be able to *[insert big benefit]*. You'll also be able to *[insert more benefits]*.

Sounds great, doesn't it?

But don't take my word for it. Here's what other members from all over the country are saying about *[insert Coaching Program name]*.

People want proof... so give it to them as testimonials. Remember when I said earlier that you're going to use your Launch Members (aka the people you let into your membership first for free) as testimonials? Make sure to ask them for a review. And when you get your Founding Members, ask them for testimonials too. Keep building your database of testimonials so you'll constantly be able to have stories to tell how your membership is making a difference in people's lives.

*[insert testimonial]*

*[insert testimonial]*

*[insert testimonial]*

You're going to use a number of bullet points to describe the benefits of your membership. Think about it next and make a list. What are the benefits of your membership?

## Which Of These Powerful Secrets Could You Use To [*Insert Benefit*]?

- *Bullet*
- *Bullet*
- *Bullet*
- *Bullet*
- *Bullet*
- *Bullet*
- *Bullet*
- *Bullet*
- ...And a whole lot more!

Most people will say things like, "You're going to get a membership site. You're going to get an online community. You're going to get a private Facebook group. You're going to get tools." These *aren't benefits*... they're features.

Instead, think about the outcomes that matter to your ideal member. For example, the bullet point describing the outcome of a membership site might say:

- *You're going to get a private online portal where you will easily and conveniently be able to access the tools you need to get – a one-stop shop, where you can discover how quickly and easily you can lose weight.*

See how I never said "Membership Site"? Instead, it's an "online portal" that's going to provide the member with convenience.

Again, make every bullet point provide a *benefit* that's *outcome-oriented*, not simply "here's the membership site, the Facebook group, all of that." It's the outcome of those things that matters.

Next you'll get into the investment required for your membership.

### Okay, So What's The Investment For *[insert problem they'll be eliminating]* Forever!!

You see, there are many people who spend *[insert exorbitant cost]* trying to *[insert problem to be solved]*. Not to mention the countless hours of time wasted banging your head against the wall.

Plus you can join other memberships that range between *[insert cost]* and *[insert cost]* but still end up frustrated at the end.

Believe me, I used to be there!

But I'm not going to charge you anywhere near that amount for *[insert Coaching Program name]*. You can get everything you need to *[solve problem]* and *[insert benefits]* for a low monthly investment of *[insert price of Coaching Program]*.

You see, *[$]* is a drop in the bucket compared to the money you're going to waste on ineffective *[whatever they're doing that's not solving the problem]*. You probably spend that much on *[insert frivolous stuff they buy—like Starbucks lattes, magazines, movie rentals, etc.]* that are gone in an instant.

Why not invest that money to *[insert benefit]* instead?

Believe me, I wish I had *[insert Coaching Program name]* when I was *[insert situation you were going through in story above]*. It would have saved me hours of frustrating trial and error so I can *[insert benefit]*.

So what's the catch? Why am I practically giving this coaching program away?

We'll, it's really quite simple. I want to give everyone, including you, the ability to *[insert problem to be solved]*. I definitely wouldn't have been able to *[insert benefit]* without it!

Of course, you'll want to mention the bonuses you're including for becoming a Founding Member (or what have you).

In fact, to shamelessly bribe you even further, here are:

## *[#]* FREE Bonuses
## Worth *[$]* If You Take
## Action Right NOW!

**FREE Bonus Gift #1**: [Explain bonus and give value]
**FREE Bonus Gift #2**: [Explain bonus and give value]
**FREE Bonus Gift #3**: [Explain bonus and give value]

That's right! I'll give you these *[#]* bonuses worth *[$]* when you take action today and invest in *[Coaching Program]*. This is a limited time offer I can take down at any second—so take action today!

Now it's time for the part about your Guarantee. We've talked about this previously, so I'm not going to go into a lot of detail now, but make sure to put it in the letter so they know it's there.

## But I Know You're Skeptical
## About *[Insert Big Benefit]* In As
## Short Amount Of Time Possible!

That's OK... I've been there! Before undergoing *[insert the pain you described in your story]* I felt the same way.

That's why I'm offering the following 100% Risk Free Guarantee:

I personally guarantee that if you don't *[insert benefit or problem to be solved]* in *[insert guarantee length]* then let me know and I'll issue a prompt and courteous refund for your most recent monthly investment. No questions asked—no hassles!

I feel this is as fair as I could be!

That means you can try out *[Coaching Program]* at my risk. See if it works for you or not. And if it doesn't produce, I honestly want you to ask for your money back!!

But I'm sure you'll be able to *[solve problem and insert benefit]* in no time. I wouldn't have spent the time and effort creating *[insert Coaching Program name]* and writing this letter to you if I didn't think it would *[insert benefit]!*

Now we come to the closing, where you give the call to action and sign off. It's all right here in this template.

### You Really Can't Afford NOT To Invest In *[Coaching Program]!*

Right now, you have two choices:

You can either *[insert problems they're having and pain it is causing in their lives]*.

Or you can take action today, right now, by investing in *[Coaching Program]*. And start *[insert benefits and how their lives are going to be better after using this Coaching Program]*.

This choice is yours.

Imagine *[insert detailed, colorful description of how their lives are going to be better and how their pain is going to disappear after they use your Coaching Program]*.

You can start *[solving this problem]* instantly when you take action and order *[Coaching Program]*.

You've got to have a call to action. You want to be able to say in your letter, "click this button to sign up now," or "go here to sign up." Give them that call to action, especially with your Founding Member rate – as in, "Go here now to become a Founding Member and lock in the lowest rate ever for this membership."

So sign up today, right now, while it's still hot on your mind. And be prepared to *[big benefit they want]!*

Sincerely,

*[Your Name]*

Lastly, we have the PS and the PPS.

Are you wondering why you need to include a PS and a PPS? Because this is a sales letter, some people will not read every single word. Many, many people will skim through the headlines and subheads, then they will read the closing, and then they'll head straight to the PS and the PPS.

> P.S. One more thing, it's important: I reserve the right to raise the price of *[Coaching Program]* based on demand. Plus, the *[#]* bonuses worth *[$]* may be taken off this and sold individually. So invest in *[Coaching Program]* while this offer is still up!

> P.P.S. Imagine being able to *[insert big benefit they want and how their life will be better]*. *[Coaching Program]* was created to enable you to *[solve problem and get the big benefit]* as fast as possible. The best part is you're backed by my *[insert guarantee]*. Go here to sign up today!

This is where again, you restate your offer just right in the PS and PPS – and one more thing, make sure to talk about the benefits and give them that final call to action.

## Create a Dual Readership Path

When writing this letter, you want to create what's called a "dual readership path." That means you give a couple of ways for people to read your letter – for those who read every word and for those who only skim looking for the high points that stand out.

The people who skim through your letter and go through it piece by piece will read:

- The headline
- The copy here and there
- The name of the membership
- They might stop after seeing some of the testimonials and read those.
- They're definitely going to read the bullets. "Hmmm, which of these could I use?"
- And then they'll skim on until they hit the bonuses they will receive if they sign up.

- They'll see the guarantee and think, "Yeah, I'm a little skeptical," and read the guarantee.
- Then they definitely read the PS and the PPS.

That's dual readership. You will guide them along the way by formatting key points you want to communicate. Big, bold headlines and sub-headlines. Big testimonials with real names and probably people's pictures. Bonuses that are italicized so they stick out more. Bullet points that are bold and formatted differently.

We want to include those elements of dual readership so that people can skim the page. Because many people *will*.

You might say, "Well, Scott, that's a long sales letter. Is everybody going to read it?"

Yes. Some people will read it. Others will skim it. You want to appeal to them both.

## Make the Letter As Good As It Can Be

Consider including a video with your sales letter. If you do this, a good location is at the top of the sales letter. It could be just you sharing your story about why you created this membership. It could also be you reading back the sales letter to them, word for word.

If you use video, you don't want to make it look like you're reading. Just talk to the camera and tell them the sales letter.

Make sure you have a deadline. Again. I mentioned this previously so I'm not going to belabor it, but you need to give deadlines for your offer.

Remember to create scarcity, as in "Only the next 10 people who sign up will get these bonuses."

Use graphics. But you also don't want to overuse them, so use them sparingly. I usually like to use graphics for testimonials, where I include a face, along with city and state if possible. I might also include graphics for bonuses or for a free gift. Then I might include a graphic for the guarantee, and one with the name of the membership as a branding thing. But don't insert graphics everywhere. They have to make sense and serve a purpose.

By the way, breaking up your sales page with graphics is *not* serving the purpose. Your visuals have to continue to engage the reader to continue to move forward. They have to speak to and coincide with what you're trying to convey. You want the graphics to make sense. Don't put a cute graphic in there just to be cute. Aim for clarity over cute. I don't care if it's a cute sales page. What I want to know is, "Did it convert? Did people actually sign up from it?" Regardless of looks, is your sales page actually getting people to take action and sign up?

After you write your sales letter, I want you to proofread by reading it aloud. Literally read that sales letter out loud… word for word… because in your mind when you're proofing things, you unconsciously insert words where there might not be any words. I want you to read it out loud, one word at a time, because then you'll catch typos, missing words, and more.

## Make Sure Your Sales System Works

Along with making sure your sales letter is as good as it can be, make sure to test the functionality of the technology involved with selling people into your membership.

Before you get anybody to sign up, you should go through the sign-up process first to make sure that everything is set up correctly.

- Make sure that your recurring billing is set up correctly, and that the functionality actually works.

- Make sure you know where the sales page is going to send them after they sign up.

- Verify that your credit card processor is functioning correctly and actually captures the money.

- Then I want you to walk away and check everything again.

I told my team to never send out a sales page without first pulling out our own credit card and testing the process. I mean, I can refund myself. I can refund my team. It costs me nothing to do that.

Walk through the entire process first and then put it out there for people to sign up.

## Take this Sales Letter and Make It Your Own

This sales letter template has been built for you. Take it, use it. Millions of dollars have been generated from it and I'm giving it to you so that you can use it.

I know not all the language may sound right in your head or like the way you speak, so make it yours. Adjust it to fit your personality and use your own words.

But follow the format. Don't violate the format!

This is direct response marketing and it's worked for years. It may not look pretty, but it will convert.

That's what you want. You want results, because results rule when it comes to selling your membership. Forget about cute and pretty and graphically designed.

It's all about being clear and getting results.

---

If you would like a free copy of the
"High-Ticket Coaching Sales Letter Swipe File"
all you have to do is go to

**www.FastLaunchCoach.com**

and get your editable Word document.
Plus, you'll receive
over $675.97 in bonus resources and tools.

---

# Part 4

# **T**urn Up the Volume and Demand

Turn Up the Volume and Demand

**S**cale Your Sales Without Selling

**A**ttract Your Right-Fit Members

**F**ind What Your Audience Desires to Join Now

# 14 | THE 30-DAY LAUNCH CHECKLIST

I'm now going to share with you how to turn up the volume and demand for your membership by completing your *30-Day F.A.S.T. Launch Checklist.* I've created this list so you can easily set a deadline for when you're going to launch your membership and then work backwards to get everything done without stressing out.

Get your free editable copy of the *30-Day F.A.S.T. Launch Checklist* at www.FastLaunchCoach.com. Plus, you'll receive additional bonus resources and tools to help you Launch F.A.S.T.!

| DAY | GOAL | DETAILS | DATE COMPLETE? |
|-----|------|---------|----------------|
| 1 | Set your "Why" | Clarify "why" you're doing this and how you will impact people | |
| 2 | The "What" | Complete your "Content Catalog," with "Content Categories" and your first 3-month "Content Calendar" | |
| 3 | The "Who" | Clarify your "Ideal Prospective Member" using the "Secret Audience Formula" | |
| 4 | Attract Your Prospects | Set up social media to attract people using your "Prospect Attraction Tool" | |

| | | | |
|---|---|---|---|
| 5 | Invite Your "Launch Members" | Make some private invitations to join your membership for free | |
| 6 | Set up your delivery system | Choose your "membership site" (Free Facebook Group, Basic Membership Platform, or Advanced Membership Site Software) | |
| 7 | "Prove Your Membership" | Get feedback from your "Launch Members" | |
| 8 | Create Buzz Plan | Create your marketing schedule for the next 14 days. | |
| 9 | Buzz Day 1 | Promote to your email audience and social media | |
| 10 | Buzz Day 2 | Promote to your email audience and social media | |
| 11 | Buzz Day 3 | Promote to your email audience and social media | |
| 12 | Buzz Day 4 | Promote to your email audience and social media | |
| 13 | Buzz Day 5 | Promote to your email audience and social media | |
| 14 | Buzz Day 6 | Promote to your email audience and social media | |
| 15 | Buzz Day 7 | Promote to your email audience and social media | |
| 16 | Founding Member Launch + Bonuses | Invite your audience to your new membership! | |

HIGH-TICKET COACH

| 17 | Founding Member Launch + Bonuses | Invite your audience to your new membership! | |
|---|---|---|---|
| 18 | Founding Member Launch + Bonuses | Invite your audience to your new membership! | |
| 19 | Founding Member Launch + Bonuses | Invite your audience to your new membership! | |
| 20 | Founding Member Launch + Bonuses | Invite your audience to your new membership! | |
| 21 | Founding Member Launch + BONUSES END TODAY | Invite your audience to your new membership! | |
| 22 | Founding Member Launch (no bonuses) | Invite your audience to your new membership! | |
| 23 | Founding Member Launch (no bonuses) | Invite your audience to your new membership! | |
| 24 | Founding Member Launch (no bonuses) | Invite your audience to your new membership! | |
| 25 | Founding Member Launch (no bonuses) | Invite your audience to your new membership! | |
| 26 | Founding Member Launch (no bonuses) | Invite your audience to your new membership! | |
| 27 | Founding Member Launch Ends (no bonuses) | Invite your audience to your new membership! | |

143

| 28 | CELEBRATE! | | |
|----|------------|---|---|
| 29 | Continue to Deliver Value to Your Members | | |
| 30 | Develop Your Next Buzz Campaign and Your Next Membership Promotion | | |

## How to Use the Checklist

First off, you've got some of these things done already! We've talked through creating your Content Catalog, identifying your right-fit member, and attracting those prospects. Hopefully you've already created your written notes from previous chapters.

That's a big portion you can mark as "complete."

Here's what I want you to do next...

SET A DEADLINE

Scroll to Day 27 – Founding Member Launch Ends Today (no bonuses).

That date is the deadline for when your Founding Member launch will end. Insert a date right there in that column, and that gives you an endpoint from which you work backwards.

For example, if you set your Founding Member launch deadline to be the 30th of the month, then you just work your way back and set dates based off that one.

You'll then have a complete marketing plan for everything that needs to get done. Once you have your Founding Member launch date nailed down, you'll be able to set up all of your promotions, emails, and interactions leading up to that moment.

For now, what I want you to do *right at this very moment* is schedule every single date based on that deadline. Write in the dates of each particular promotion!

## CREATE BUZZ

On Days 8 through 15 you'll be creating a 7-day buzz campaign. In the next chapter I'll detail how to create that buzz campaign and leverage your social media to attract members to your membership. For now, just mark in the dates and trust the system.

## CELEBRATE

Another thing I want you to highlight is Day 28 – Celebrate!

I really do want you to celebrate. I want you to write down how you will reward yourself when you successfully launch your membership. It could be a financial reward – perhaps you're going to treat yourself to some sort of purchase. It could be a vacation. It could be all sorts of things, maybe even just taking time with your family and rewarding them for their support of you during this process.

You know, when I hit a certain point in my business, I took my family for a 10-day trip to New York City. We flew first-class, stayed in really nice hotels, and went to three Broadway shows. We had the full experience with black cars shuttling us around, to and from the airport. It was really nice. We even ate at some of the best restaurants in all of New York.

That was one of the ways I chose to reward myself for getting to a certain point in my business.

It wasn't just something I wanted to do for me. I wanted to create memories for my whole family. This was important to me because I could sense my daughters would soon be grown up and should get to have a special experience before they left home.

I created that experience not only as a reward for me, but also for my family.

Take a moment to consider what it is that you would like to do to celebrate and reward yourself for launching your membership. Forget about details of how many members... just celebrate the fact that you got it done, the fact that you've been waiting to launch your membership, you've chosen to do this, and it's actually out there where it can change the world.

## KEEP DELIVERING VALUE TO MORE AND MORE MEMBERS

On Day 29 you'll see the reminder to continue delivering value to your members. That will be ongoing. It's not just one day, that's an ongoing thing you will do.

On Day 30, I encourage you to "Develop your next buzz campaign and your next membership promotion." Don't rest on your laurels! Start planning your next membership promotion to keep bringing in new members.

## Get This Done

I've created this *30-Day F.A.S.T. Launch Checklist* to let you know you *can* do this in 30 days. It *is* possible.

I know your desire to launch your own membership has been something you've been wanting to do for months, if not years.

And I'm giving you a blueprint for how you can do it in the next 30 days.

When you launch your new membership, it doesn't matter how many members you get, it just matters that you have finally brought this to fruition. You've accomplished something!

Over the next 30 days, follow this checklist step-by-step. Get it done. Mark it complete. I look forward to celebrating with you on the launch of your brand-new membership!

# 15 | THE 14-DAY BUZZ CAMPAIGN

Let's dive in to create your 14-day Social Media Buzz Campaign.

If you're like me, you have this love/hate relationship with social media. Whenever I open Facebook, LinkedIn, or any social media channel, I look at the screen and say, "Okay, what should I post today?"

I'm a systems guy. *Systems* are anything that will save me stress, time, energy, or money. For me, I figure, "Well, if I'm going to have to do this every day – interact and post – why not come up with a system?"

I'm going to share with you the very simple system I like to use to mix up everything on social media.

## 10 Different Posts That Will Get People to Like, Share, and Take Action

What follows are 10 post types that will help you get interaction on social media – meaning people will like them, share them, comment on them, and take action.

This campaign is about creating awareness for your membership launch. It's not really meant to create sales directly through your social media channels, because you haven't launched yet. For now you're just creating a buzz, which is what you want to do at this point in the process.

### 1. THE QUOTE

First is the quote post. Here's an example of something I shared. You can send it perhaps in an email, but it's simply meant to be a nice little "Mindset Monday" sort of saying.

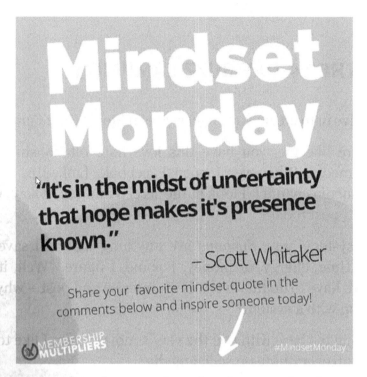

"It's in the midst of uncertainty that hope makes its presence known."

I shared this during the height of the pandemic, when everybody was experiencing a great deal of uncertainty. Notice the little call to action there at the bottom, asking people to share their favorite mindset quote in the comments.

Again, does it say anything about membership? No. It's designed to build interaction and get people to take notice inside of social media.

## 2. THE ANNOUNCEMENT

The announcement post is interesting because it's actually something you can do as a Facebook feature. Here's an example from one of my private groups. Just mark the post as an "announcement."

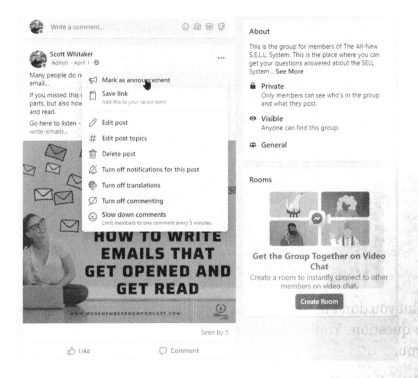

When you mark a post as an announcement, everybody inside your Facebook group will be able to see it. Facebook gives it priority. Literally, when you mark it as an announcement, it pops to the top of your Facebook page and Facebook feed.

## 3. THE QUESTION

Then we have the question post.

"What's your biggest challenge when it comes to growing your membership?"

Designed as an image, it can look like:

But you don't have to be fancy on this. You can literally just post a question. You're simply trying to get people to interact with you.

Something that's interesting is you can actually use your question as a way to identify your ideal prospective members.

One of the things you might consider doing is posting a question to make sure you're able to speak directly to your right-fit members. For instance, if you think that your right-fit members have a particular struggle, you might ask, "Which of these do you struggle with most? This one or that one?"

Another one I like to use is: "What's your biggest struggle when you are trying to get more members?" Just substitute your own niche's pain points when you ask this question.

People commented on that question, and I was able to confirm (or learn) that they were struggling with their marketing, or with social media, or with email, or with knowing how to do this or that. Then I could use that feedback to improve the effectiveness of my marketing.

## 4. THE INVITE

Then there's the invite, which looks this:

This post invites people to schedule a free strategy session.

I provided a little bit of commentary, and then a GIF to make it even more eye-catching. It's all about inviting people to a strategy session.

Even if you're not offering free strategy sessions, you can still invite people into your Facebook group. You could invite people to "like your business page." You could invite people to use your prospect attraction tool. You could invite people to do all sorts of things.

Use this type of post as an opportunity to create buzz around your membership launch.

## 5. THE GIVEAWAY

Then there's the giveaway. For my launch, I made a little talking-head Scott. "You're invited to join me for free training."

The post that went with the image said essentially, "We're going to do this free training where you can discover how you can launch FAST using one simple strategy, so go and sign up for this free training now."

I invited people to be a part of that.

Now, if you're doing a giveaway for your prospect attraction tool (like a free report, a webinar, or whatever you've created to get people to sign up on your list), this post type would be appropriate.

An advanced strategy on this would be to go inside your group, create an event, and invite all your followers to come and be part of that online event. (That's a little bonus for you when it comes to creating events inside your Facebook group.)

## 6. THE MEME

Then there's the meme post. I used this post type to invite a few select people to a free event, essentially giving a trial run to parts of the system I would eventually turn into my membership.

Notice how I build in questions that allow someone to determine if they're right for this particular offer. And I used scarcity (limited spots) to drive urgency.

Again, I just have a little eye-catching GIF and a call to action, where it invites just five people who want to launch a membership during a 2-day live training... and they must be willing to commit to a specific set of requirements I mention in the post, so I can help identify my right-fit members.

This also encourages prospects to willingly commit themselves to a higher level of participation, simply because they agreed ahead of time that they would.

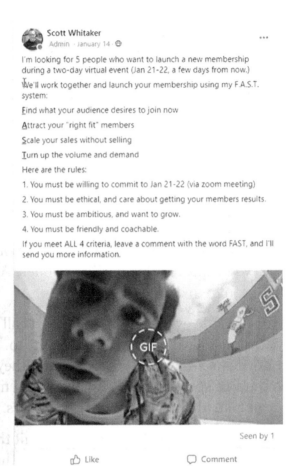

Scott Whitaker
Admin · January 14

I'm looking for 5 people who want to launch a new membership during a two-day virtual event (Jan 21-22, a few days from now.)

We'll work together and launch your membership using my F.A.S.T. system:

Find what your audience desires to join now

Attract your "right fit" members

Scale your sales without selling

Turn up the volume and demand

Here are the rules:

1. You must be willing to commit to Jan 21-22 (via zoom meeting)

2. You must be ethical, and care about getting your members results.

3. You must be ambitious, and want to grow.

4. You must be friendly and coachable.

If you meet ALL 4 criteria, leave a comment with the word FAST, and I'll send you more information.

Seen by 1

👍 Like          💬 Comment

## 7. THE "SHARE" POST (OTHER PEOPLE'S CONTENT)

A share post is just want it sounds like. You share someone else's content. You might say something like, "Hey, I read this article *[or book or whatever]* and wanted to share it with you." Then simply share that content into your social media post.

This is another way of becoming an authority, by creating affinity with your audience and providing value to them.

## 8. THE POLL

Then there's the poll post. I asked my tribe, "How would you like to consume content?" and offered choices A, B, C, or D.

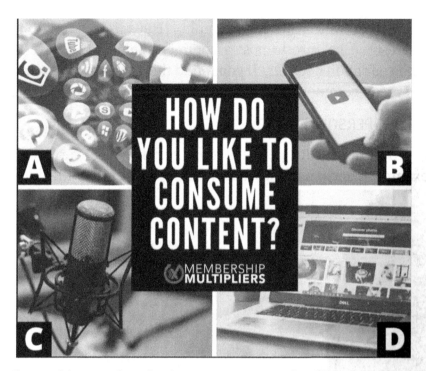

I threw this together for an event we were leading, but if I was to redo it today, I would probably use a poll type where viewers click on one of three buttons.

You could create a poll that asks: "Which of these best describes you?" and then have three choices that help identify where someone is along the process of dealing with whatever pain point you're hoping to solve. "I'm just getting started," "I'm making progress, but it feels slow," or "I'm ready to go, I just need to find the time."

In the image above, I simply asked people to post their answers in the comments, but now Facebook offers the ability to create a poll with options so people can choose from multiple answers.

## 9. THE "SOCIAL" POST (LIKE, COMMENT, OR SHARE)

A social post is simply one where you tell people to like, comment, or share something you've posted. The goal is to get interaction with you, for example, "Hey, if you found this interesting, be sure to post a comment below and share this with your audience." Or "If you found this free resource helpful, be sure to comment and share."

## 10. THE PERSONAL POST

Finally, there's the personal post and here's a very simple example from something that was happening in my life:

My youngest daughter just graduated from high school. One of my traditions is to take my new graduate to breakfast to have some father-daughter time.

This post allowed me to show some personality by being a bit more open than I normally would be. It was also an opportunity to share a victory that my family was celebrating.

OTHER OPTIONS

You now have 10 different types of posts to get you started, but there are still other options that Facebook offers.

For example, you can create a "room," where you host a Q&A, or perhaps ask for recommendations. You can create a "live" video, by going live inside your Facebook group or on your business page or on your profile.

Whatever post style speaks to you most right now, go ahead and choose one... and create it!

## Planning Out Your 14-Day Buzz Campaign

Create a table like this on paper or in a spreadsheet to lay out the plan for your 14-day campaign.

| 14 Day Buzz Plan | | | |
|---|---|---|---|
| DAY | SOCIAL MEDIA POST TYPE | POST COPY | COMPLETE? |
| 1 | | | |
| 2 | | | |
| 3 | | | |
| 4 | | | |
| 5 | | | |
| 6 | | | |
| 7 | | | |
| 8 | | | |
| 9 | | | |
| 10 | | | |
| 11 | | | |
| 12 | | | |
| 13 | | | |
| 14 | | | |

To make your plan, do something like the following:

On Day 1, post a quote.

On Day 2, make an announcement that you're about to launch a brand-new membership.

On Day 3, post a question to learn more about your prospect.

On Day 4, do a giveaway of your prospect attraction tool.

On Day 5, share something a bit more personal.

Then mix it up on the days that follow.

What you'll begin to see is that without too much trouble you can easily fill all 14 days, ready and done, by maybe adding another quote here or there, asking a question about your prospect, or posting a poll.

It's a system. You can just rotate these over and over. Eventually you won't even have to think about this.

Yes, I may have to come up with fresh content in the future, but for me I know that on the 1st and 15th I'm always going to use a quote post. It makes it very simple for me. No more opening up Facebook, staring at the screen, then trying to figure out what to post. This gives you a simple process you can follow.

---

Get your free copy of the 14-Day Buzz Campaign

**www.FastLaunchCoach.com**

to download the editable version.
Plus, you'll receive additional bonus resources and tools to help you Launch F.A.S.T.!

---

## Advanced Strategy

For an advanced strategy, *repurpose* your email content and post it on social media. Take your email copy and simply craft it in such a way that you can also post it on Facebook, or Twitter, or Instagram, or LinkedIn... wherever your right-fit member is hanging out.

For example, I recently wrote an email making the point that growing your business means asking the right questions. I sent this email out to my list. Then I thought, "You know, that'd be a really good post for my social media."

I took that exact content, then edited it a bit to make it look like a post. I grabbed a little GIF image to go with it as a visual attention grabber, and ran it. Take your emails and put them on your social media.

You might say, "Scott, you know, the people on my social media are the same people on my email list."

Here's why you want to do this anyway. Have you checked your email open rates? It may be 20-25%. Let's just be generous for a moment and say it's 25%. That means only 1 out of every 4 people opened your email, which in turn means 3 out of 4 people did not see your brilliant content at all.

Here's what I know... If I take that same email and put it out on social media, the 3 people who didn't see it in email are far more likely to see it.

Therefore, when you market by email, plan to use that same content and recraft it so that it works as a Facebook post. Plus, you can do this for LinkedIn and all the other platforms immediately. Repurpose it for all your social media channels.

This one technique is going to dramatically expand the number of eyeballs you get on your marketing. Instead of having only a 20-25% open rate on your emails, you're going to attract more people to your content via other channels.

Take these strategies, implement them, rotate them. Don't let this 14-Day Buzz Campaign be something you use only once. Make it ongoing to stay connected and continue to attract your ideal prospects and future right-fit members.

You can literally just rotate these different kinds of posts over and over, creating new ones for social media channels as you send emails to your tribe. You'll never have to wonder again about what you're going to put out on social media.

It's time to get started creating this campaign, and getting people interested in your membership and what you have to offer them. Plan out your first 14 days of posts and see how easy it can be!

# 16 | NEVER STOP MARKETING

As you turn up the volume and create buzz and demand for your membership... getting in front of more and more of your right-fit members... it's important that you *never stop marketing* your membership.

There's the acronym ABS, Always Be Selling, but I prefer Always Be Marketing, because marketing isn't always about selling. Marketing can also be about providing value and building relationships with your prospects.

The challenge lies in making that happen *consistently.*

## A Failure to Communicate

What happens all too often is you open up your computer, hoping to write an email to send to your audience, or to create a post for your social media. But then you get stuck because you're just not sure what to write.

I don't want you to be panicked about this. Since I'm all about systems, let's save you stress, time, energy, and money with my simple system to keep your membership program in front of your ideal prospective members through email.

First I want you to realize something important...

You may already have an email list right now, but it's *possible* that you've not been sending regular email to this audience. The problem of not staying in regular touch is that you lose credibility with your audience.

I saw somebody post in a Facebook group recently that it had been three months since they'd logged into their CRM. Come to find out, somebody or some glitch had totally deleted all of their contacts.

I remember thinking, honestly, those contacts might as well have been deleted because if that person hadn't communicated in over three months, they've almost certainly lost all credibility.

Think about it. If you last received an email three months ago from someone you met online and downloaded something from, when their name suddenly appears in your inbox you might be wondering, "Why am I getting this email? *Who is this person?*"

Studies show that by emailing your audience more frequently, you'll actually increase the engagement with them through your email marketing.

But the emails you send have to be good ones. (And I'm going to give you examples of how to make sure your emails are really good.) When you only email your audience once every 2 or 3 weeks, decreasing your engagement with them, your open rates actually decrease as well.

Ultimately you end up getting more and more opt-outs from your list. And when people do open your email, they wonder, "Who is this person?" They then opt-out as well.

A lot of people out there are fearful of opt-outs, and I get it, but you don't need to be afraid of them. When somebody opts out of my list, I'm grateful because they've identified themself as somebody I'm not going to be able to help.

Having said that, when you don't communicate regularly, you lose out on converting the prospects who were your right-fit people into future members. Let that be a driving factor to motivate you to send out better emails so you can get more members.

Next I'll give you a simple process to create your email marketing calendar, using four different types of emails that consistently provide value to your audience, build your relationships, and convert people into your membership.

This system takes the guesswork out of creating those emails, and allows you to do it consistently so you can benefit the most from your hard work.

## The Content Email

The Content Email is meant to teach and demonstrate your expertise. It's an authority builder. It gives you credibility in the eyes of your audience by providing really good content.

Consider it almost like a blog post or article, but in an email format that demonstrates your expertise.

Why should you send this? First, because it will build authority and demonstrate that you have a membership worth giving a try.

When somebody receives this kind of email, you want them to say, "Wow, this was really good. If they gave away this content for free in an email, how much more would they teach in their membership? How much more could I learn? What greater desire might I get fulfilled just by being in the membership?"

When I started out in email marketing with this business, I only had 50 people on my list. But I had one person who found so much value in my emails that he forwarded them to 20-plus other people. And one of those people became a 6-figure paying client of mine... just because I had demonstrated the authority and quality of content I could provide... in a free email.

Let that sink in.

I'm not saying you're going to get a 6-figure member out of an email you send, but I am saying that when people find value in what you're sending out there for free, they'll be more likely to believe there's greater value in something they would have to pay for. What's interesting is that I didn't even have a call to action in that email. The person just found so much value in it that he forwarded it to some people he knew and one of them reached out to me.

In this email, you can create it like an article or blog post, teaching right inside the copy. You can also share other people's content and talk about it (while giving them credit, of course), provide a commentary on it, tell people the value you found in it, and offer step-by-step directions.

Here's an example from one of my content emails:

> Hey John,
>
> It's one of the issues we don't like when it comes to running a membership business...
>
> Members canceling!
>
> Sometimes cancelations can feel personal, as if you did something wrong.
>
> Sometimes cancelations cause you to doubt the value of what you provide.
>
> Sometimes cancelations cause you to wonder if your pricing is just right.
>
> When you start that downward spiral, you begin to make decisions based off of bad information. And then you do even more damage to your membership business.
>
> But I've got GOOD NEWS.
>
> You can get your FREE copy of "Why People Quit Your Membership Program & What You Can Do About It."
>
> Click here to download your FREE copy now!

> You'll get many tips and tools that I've personally used to grow a membership from 72 to over 3,000 members, personally handling cancelation requests and training staff members and other membership businesses to do the same.
>
> There are no forms to fill out, just click the link and you'll be taken to the page to download it.

As you can see, I was giving away a free e-book. The email was intended to build authority and provide content to my audience and give away a free strategy guide. I offered some reasons why they should download it and take advantage of the opportunity.

What are some content ideas you have for your emails? Could you write an article? Give step-by-step instructions? Maybe share and offer commentary on someone else's content?

## The Soft-Pitch Email

The soft-pitch email is a content email that contains a call to action for people to take a next step. It's not a targeted campaign with a hard sell. Instead, it's just a subtle offer for someone to take action.

It also builds your authority and gives your audience a next step to take with you.

Here's a sample of what I like to add at the end of my email:

If you're ready to multiply your membership and money, here are four more ways we can work together!

1. Get a FREE copy of *Accelerate: How to Get Your Next 10, 100, 500 or Even 1,000 Members...* Yes, you can get a free copy of my brand-new book! In it, you discover more on how to promote your membership, get more members and increase retention.

Go here to get your free book now!

2. The Membership Accelerators Club... This is the place for membership businesses looking for marketing tools that you can plug and play to get more members. Literally, these tools will help you promote your program and get more members.

Go here to learn more now (and get the 4-Day Membership Generator!)

3. Are You Looking to Reduce Cancellations and Keep More Members... If you really care about your members, why not try to RESCUE THEM and help them with your membership? Your membership could possibly be the very tool that helps them get beyond their trouble, tension or transition.

Go here to help more people and keep them paying!

4. Are you interested in working together to multiply your membership? One of my clients just sold $160K in memberships. If you're interested in learning more about how we may be able to work together... just REPLY to this message and put "PRIVATE CLIENT" in the subject line... tell me a little about your membership and what you'd like to work on together, and let's see if and how I can help.

This soft-pitch example showed the four ways that I could help someone. (It would be worthwhile for you to come up with four ways that you can help your prospects too.)

1. Get my book
2. Join the membership
3. Pick up a resource
4. Accept a high-ticket offer

Remember, it's not a hard pitch. It doesn't have a deadline. There is no scarcity, no bonuses, none of that. Just an opportunity to let someone determine their next step with you.

So, what are some soft-pitch ideas that you have? Write them down! What are four ways people can work with you? What are four ways you can help people take a next step?

When it comes to promoting, many times marketers just want to say, "Marry me, marry me, marry me. Join my membership, join my membership!"

But no one wants to get married if you've only just met or had one date. Instead, let your prospects take time to get to know you by offering a few ways they can do that. Let them choose the path that's best for them.

## The Hard-Pitch Email

This email is all about giving people a clear call to action. This email has a deadline, and it's one of a group of emails.

You want to send this email to grow your membership, sell your products, and get people to buy. Often it's one element of a campaign that drives toward your deadline when "time's running out."

Your Founding Membership marketing campaign will fall into this category. You will say, "Sign up before DATE and become a Founding Member." You'll make your offer like we talked about in the sales letter earlier, offer your bonuses, and your guarantee, and remind people about that ticking deadline.

There are also other times where you might use this kind of email:

- Webinar sales email sequence

- A holiday sale, such as Thanksgiving or Labor Day, or where there's a long weekend opportunity to sell.

- For a trial offer – "Get your first 30 days for half price" or "Get 4 Weeks for $4"

Here's an example I used on my 45th birthday:

---

Have you ever considered who was the first person to celebrate their birthday?

If you think about it, we should all be grateful for that person. Imagine people getting the first birthday invitation to celebrate the day of someone's birth. HA!

We'll never know who that person was, but here are five fun facts about birthdays:

* Egyptians celebrated birthdays for their gods.

* The Greeks were the first to add candles to a cake to celebrate.

* The Romans were the first to celebrate birthdays for common people.

* Contemporary birthday cakes were invented by German bakers.

* The "Happy Birthday" song was a remix of "Good Morning to All"

So, why all the birthday fun facts?

Well, tomorrow is my 45th birthday!

And to celebrate, my team thought it would be a fun gesture to give you a test-drive of the Membership Accelerators Club – four weeks for $5 and receive over $997 in bonuses and resources!

See what they did: 4-5! I wasn't too sure about sharing my age, but I decided if it gives us an opportunity to help you and your members, why not?

Click the link below to find out more:

www.MembershipMultipliers.com/45

---

We ran this promotion for two days, starting on Thursday, and then obviously Friday was the midnight deadline.

And we picked up members from this.

---

P.S. One last thing, in all seriousness, I'm also raising funds for Compassion International to help expectant moms and mothers of newborns to provide for the care of their babies. Just my way of giving back on my birthday. Go here to donate to the cause!

P.P.S. If you sign up for the Membership Accelerators Club, I'm going to make a donation in your honor. I'll be doing it for all the members of the Membership Accelerators Club. You can actually make two contributions, donate here and join the Membership Accelerator Club here.

Get your 4 weeks for $5 now and receive over $997.00 in bonuses and resources!

Scott Whitaker
Author & Founder of Membership Multipliers

---

I used this email to get people to take action on joining the membership, *plus* raise money for a good cause. It was motivated out of generosity, so it's not something you necessarily have to imitate.

In this example of a hard-pitch email, I noted what was being offered – 4 weeks for $5, at a $997 value – and I gave a deadline and a call to action.

What are some hard-pitch email ideas you could use? Write them down!

Maybe it's your own birthday. Maybe there's a holiday coming up and you could do a 2-day flash sale of your membership. Take a moment and write out some of those email ideas now.

## The Nurture Email

This one is called the nurture email because it's where you nurture your relationship with the people on your email list.

I put this at number four because I like doing it right after a hard pitch. When placed in a sequence, it lightens the mood after emails that were designed to sell, demonstrating to the audience reasons why they should continue to engage with you even if they weren't yet ready to buy during your recent promotion.

The Nurture Email is designed to help others stay connected so they can continue to receive value. Here's an example.

---

Hey Scott,

There are seven Membership Multipliers that exist in your membership program.

It doesn't matter...
... how long your membership has been around.
... how many members you have.
... how much you charge for membership.
... if you have a membership site or not.

They exist whether or not you even know it (which most don't even know their existence.)

These multipliers are there and they're at work in your program.

Your decision is: Will you leverage these multipliers to grow your members and build your membership?

You don't have to reinvent the wheel. *You just have to maximize these multipliers and let them grow your membership.*

That's why I've put together this free strategy guide:

*"Membership Multipliers:*
*Seven Proven Strategies to Multiply Your Membership & Profits"*

Click here to download your FREE copy!

---

I invite readers to download a free copy of the *Seven Membership Multipliers*, letting them know there are no strings attached, no web form to complete, no hoop to jump through. Literally just "click here to download your free copy."

But I did give a deadline because I wanted people to know they need to take action, because people don't always do what they *should* do... they do what's *urgent*. That's why we add a deadline on this type of email.

What are some nurture ideas that you have for your emails? What can you give away?

## Planning Your Email Calendar

These four types of emails become the foundation of a system you can use to stay in touch with your email list.

This is how you will never have to open up your computer and wonder, "What am I going to email my audience today?" Instead, you now have a plan you can use over and over.

Because there are usually four weeks in a month, on Week 1, you might plan to offer a content email series. If you have something like a 3-point article, on Monday, give an overview of all three points. In Tuesday's email speak just about point #1. On Wednesday, point #2. On Thursday, it's point #3. Then on Friday you should draw the conclusion.

In this way, you can quickly build an entire email series, five days' worth of emails, off that one content piece.

On Week 2, you can do the soft-pitch series in a similar way to how it worked with the content emails.

Bear in mind, I'm not saying you *must* email every weekday, Monday through Friday, but I would encourage it. It will drive engagement and keep your people connected with you.

During Week 2, share something like, "Here are four ways we can work together." Then each subsequent email that week talks about one of those four ways in more detail.

The following week can be for the hard-pitch emails. That's where you drive to a deadline. *Get these bonuses. Sign up now. Take action.*

This leads into your campaign so you're attracting members and making sales all during Week 3.

Finally, in Week 4 you come back to nurture your list. "Hey, I want to give this away for free. No form to fill out, just go here and download it."

Content, soft-pitch, hard-pitch, nurture. Content, soft-pitch, hard-pitch, nurture. Follow that cycle. It gives you a system and process you can repeat with ease.

## Never Stop Marketing

You've got this. You can make it happen! Follow this four-step plan and you will continue to grow your audience and get more members.

---

To learn more about the
"4 Different Types of Emails You Should
Be Sending & When to Use Them" visit:

**www.FastLaunchCoach.com**

where you can learn more about this system
and how you can get swipe-and-deploy
email templates to help launch your coaching offer.

---

# 17 | REMEMBER YOUR WHY

Congratulations. You made it!

This could well be the most important chapter of all and here's why...

## Because Things Won't Go as Planned

There will come a time when one or more things go in a direction you didn't expect.

- Maybe, just maybe, your launch wasn't as big as you wanted it to be (after all, you're an entrepreneur and you have big dreams!).

- Maybe it went *way* bigger than you expected, but then you hit a plateau and started to decline.

- Maybe your technology still gets in the way. (As much as I don't want technology to ever stand in the way for you, sometimes it still happens.)

- Maybe something doesn't go right with your marketing... for example, your Facebook account gets shut down.

When something doesn't go the way you expected, keep this in mind:

*"If you want to be happy, set a goal that commands your thoughts, liberates your energy and inspires your hopes."* – Andrew Carnegie

It's the goal and the process of getting there that bring your spirit to life. In establishing a membership, you're setting a goal that commands your thoughts, liberates your energy, and inspires your hopes.

Take out your journal and a pen right now because I want to ask you some reflective questions. About once every quarter, I ask myself these same exact questions and write down my answers. Sometimes it's to encourage myself. Sometimes it's to motivate me to do better. Sometimes it's just so I can serve my members in a better way.

Whatever your motivation is for doing this, I want you to write down your answers to each of the following questions:

## WHAT WILL YOUR MEMBERSHIP LOOK LIKE ONE YEAR FROM NOW?

Let's dream together. It's going to be different for every person who reads this book. For some, maybe it's 10 members. For others, maybe it's 50, 100, or even 1000 members.

Don't get caught up in making comparisons. Just think about what you want your membership to look like one year from now.

## WHAT IF THE AMOUNT OF REVENUE YOU DID IN ONE QUARTER, YOU COULD DO IN JUST ONE MONTH?

What would that be like?

Imagine if a year from now you could say, "My quarterly revenue last year used to be _____," and now you can produce that in just one month instead of three.

What's that number? Write down the dollar amount.

## WHAT IF THE AMOUNT OF REVENUE YOU DID IN ONE MONTH, YOU COULD DO IN JUST ONE WEEK?

It's possible. I've seen it. I've had it happen personally, not just for my business, but in multiple other businesses of clients I've worked with.

If you could bring in the amount of revenue you earned in one month in just one week, what's that number?

Write it down in your journal.

You're not going to share this information with anybody. You're not even going to share it with me. You're doing this for you.

## WHAT IF THE AMOUNT OF REVENUE YOU DID IN ONE WEEK, YOU DID IN ONE DAY?

It's possible. Again, I've seen it happen.

A private client of mine just launched a brand-new membership level. She's had a membership business for 10 years, with 3 high levels of membership, and just decided to launch a lower level of membership to be able to serve more people.

And in one campaign of her launch, she immediately got 21 new members, and collected around $10,000.

In one day.

Granted, she has a bigger foundation since she started 10 years ago, but she started with 12 members. In her second year, it reached around 40 members. She kept going and then in year 10 with that new lower tier of membership, the amount of revenue she used to do in *one year*, she's doing in *one month*. The amount of revenue she used to do in *one month*, she's now doing in *a week*.

And I've seen the daily sales. I can tell you the amount of revenue she's doing in *one day* on some days is the amount of revenue she used to do in *one year!*

It's now a $4 million membership business and growing. It is possible!

## WHAT IF THE NUMBER OF MEMBERS YOU GAINED IN ONE QUARTER, YOU DID IN ONE MONTH?

My client above gained 21 members just within a three-day period. Remember that in her first year, she had 12.

## WHAT IF THE NUMBER OF MEMBERS YOU GAINED IN ONE MONTH, YOU DID IN JUST ONE WEEK?

How would this change your life?

## WHAT IF THE NUMBER OF MEMBERS YOU GAINED IN ONE WEEK YOU DID IN JUST ONE DAY?

It's possible. You know it is... and it leads me to this very important question...

## WHY DO SOME MEMBERSHIPS GROW AND OTHERS DON'T?

The very simple answer is they don't know how to do marketing. That's why I explained how to create your 14-Day Buzz Plan, and how to set up ongoing marketing through email campaigns, how to launch your membership with Launch Members and Founding Members – all to help get your membership set up for success, and to help you keep it running and consistently growing!

Then there's fear.

I hope I've taken away your fear – the fear of not knowing what to do, the fear of people not signing up. Once you have a system that allows you to know exactly what to do and when to **do it,** and how to attract your right-fit members, you no longer have to be afraid of these two outcomes.

That's why you use Launch Members, so you don't need to worry about whether you'll get Founding Members. The Launch Members take away the fear.

Then there's the marketing technology. Now you no longer need to stress over having the most advanced tech in the world. Just keep it very simple.

Why do some memberships grow, and others don't?

Here's the biggest reason – it's one I've often noted – and it boils down to this.

## You Have to Know Your WHY

The one thing you must know to grow your membership is your WHY.

Your *why* is what keeps you going. It's your motivation. It's unique to you. Nobody else can give it to you, but I've seen so many people give it away.

What is your reason *why* you must get more members?

Write that question down in your journal and then answer it.

You must have a strong reason *why*.

Regardless of circumstances, and regardless of what you may encounter, there are obstacles ahead. You've got to have a reason *why* that will keep you going. If there isn't a compelling enough reason *why*, then the *what* and the *how* won't even matter.

Think about that. When you have identified your reason *why*, it will drive you to wake up in the morning to grow your membership business. It's *why* you invest the time to learn everything you can about your business, *why* you do what you need to do to get past whatever challenges and setbacks get in your way. It's time you find out *why!*

## Let Me Share My WHY With You

When I left my previous membership business, I was on top. It was the largest membership organization in its niche, having a huge impact serving people all across the U.S., Canada, Europe, Asia, and all over the world.

But what would cause me to leave being on top? What became my *why*?

Someone shared something important with me over lunch one day. He said, "Scott, there comes a point in time when you'd rather leverage wisdom and knowledge than youth and energy."

When I heard that, I wrote it down in my journal.

I didn't know then that it was going to come back to me a few years later to become my reason *why*... to become what motivates me to do what I'm doing, what motivates me to put this book together for you.

> *"I would rather leverage my wisdom and knowledge than youth and energy."*

I didn't know then that I'd someday be able to share my wisdom and knowledge with others, that I'd be able to help others develop a greater sense of hope and purpose.

My *why* is unique. It's different from yours. And it established the direction for my membership business. It made me realize that I wanted to build my membership from the top down so I could impact the most people.

What do I mean by the top down? Well, I figured:

*"Why not go after the people who would pay me the most amount of money so I could provide the greatest value to them? That way I could have a greater impact on others with lower levels of membership, by providing free products, resources, and trainings. I'm going to build my membership from the top down. I have a number of private clients that I work with, who enable me to leverage my wisdom and knowledge, but who also enable me to get paid so that I can serve people who maybe are just starting out – people just starting from scratch, who have a bigger dream of helping others."*

That's why I built my coaching using a high-ticket offer.

Another part of my *why* is to be generous, keeping one eye on the Kingdom and one eye on the business world.

As I've mentioned, I used to be a full-time pastor. I'm still a "pastor at heart." I've served the local church and I believe in the local church. It's important to me that I'm able to leverage my business so that I can do other acts of generosity.

I'm not here to preach or brag or anything like that, but that's part of my reason *why*. I truly want to leverage my business so that I can be generous and make other things happen.

This is my reason *WHY*.

## What's Yours?

Maybe it has something to do with family. Maybe it has something to do with freedom. Maybe it has something to do with getting out of debt. What is your reason *why*?

Write it down, and reflect on it.

Your *why* is the one thing you must have in order to get more members.

Sure, these marketing tactics and tools that I'm giving you will help because you've got to have them in place. But you must also have this reason *why*.

If you don't, when doubt creeps in, or a lack of knowledge, or when there's a lack of understanding and you just don't know what to do, your *why* will drive you to find out what it is that you should be doing to get members.

When you have your *why*, you'll overcome fear, you'll move past any disappointment. You'll be determined because nobody can take away your *why*.

Jim Rohn said, "If you really want to do something, you'll find a way. If you don't, you'll find an excuse."

Your *why* helps you find the way – to find the way to launch, to find the way to get members, to find the way to impact more people and serve more people more deeply.

Why do some memberships grow and others do not?

This is actually the wrong question.

The right question instead is...

# 18 | WHAT'S KEEPING YOU FROM LAUNCHING YOUR HIGH-TICKET COACHING OFFER?

A lot of people think the what, the how, the fear, the marketing, the technology, or the *fill in the blank* is what is keeping them from launching their coaching offer.

But instead, when you have a strong enough reason *why*, it outweighs all of that.

When you have a strong enough reason, you will be determined to find the *what* and the *how*, and to negotiate every obstacle that might stand in your way. In fact, that's probably what brought you to this book. You said to yourself, "I've got a strong enough reason *why*. I just have to get the tools I need to launch my high-ticket offer."

And you picked up this book... read this book... *finished* this book. Congratulations, you made a great decision!

You're going to be able to launch a membership. You have the tools, and you can make it happen. Let your *why* be the motivating factor.

What is it? You don't have to share it with me, but you've got to have it.

## Commit to Launching F.A.S.T.

The first time I tried to launch a membership, I didn't have a clue as to what to do. I didn't have the F.A.S.T. framework that I've outlined in this book. I didn't have the tools or templates that I'm sharing with you at www.FastLaunchCoach.com.

I've already given you a number of ways to create and sell your high-ticket offer, and although I've given you a number of next steps, the quickest way to launch F.A.S.T. is to go to www.FastLaunchCoach.com and become a member of my high-ticket coaching.

I constantly tell my members that my business is on full display. You get to see and experience first-hand how to run a membership business by being in my membership.

If I don't practice what I preach, my members will be the first to call me out on it. Unlike many other consultants and "gurus," I've got a true membership business. I'm not just preaching to others on what they should do; I'm doing it myself.

When I make a mistake, my members get to learn from it so they can avoid the pain and costly error in their own business.

And at the same time, they get to implement the proven methods in their business and have me by their side to help them get more members.

At this point, you really have two decisions:

1. YOU CAN CONTINUE TO GO ABOUT YOUR MEMBERSHIP THROUGH "TRIAL AND ERROR."

It's a valid method. It's a method that has unfortunately cost me the most money. I didn't have the benefit of learning from someone who was solely focused on helping me get more members and increasing my recurring revenue.

I get it. It's a default for many people. Not to mention, you may have had your trust broken by others who promised you results they couldn't provide.

However, it's been my experience, and the experience of many of my members before coming to me, that the "trial and error" method will:

**Cost you more time**. You may reach your goal, but you most likely won't do it in the time frame that you're capable of because you don't have a proven process.

**Cost you more money**. Right now, you're losing out on not having members. You're losing by not being able to help them, and you're losing out on the monthly recurring revenue. For every month that goes by, it's money lost.

2. YOU CAN TAKE MY PROVEN TOOLS AND RESOURCES AND IMPLEMENT THEM IN YOUR MEMBERSHIP.

From what I've discovered, there has yet to be a membership or association that hasn't been able to get more members, or even double or triple their membership, using what I share with my members.

You're invited to become a member of the only membership that exists just for membership businesses.

Join this community and get real-time feedback on your membership business from people who are in the trenches, just like you!

Most have found that they recoup their investment with just a couple of new members joining their membership.

You get recurring revenue! The members I get you in the first month should more than pay for the membership... not to mention the members you're going to continue to get in the months to follow.

So, let's make it happen! Let's accelerate your launch so that you can achieve all that your membership business was intended to accomplish.

I look forward to seeing you on the inside at
**www.FastLaunchCoach.com**

## Next Steps

As we wind down our time together inside this book, if there's a way that I can help you, if you're ready to take the next step, I'm always looking for people that I can help further along.

Maybe you want my help in getting more members and keeping more members... maybe I could help you attract more of your right-fit members and convert them from being a prospect into becoming a member... perhaps I could help you deliver your content in such a way that gets people the outcome they desire... or help you fully understand and embrace what it is that makes your membership unique so you can then scale it.

If there's ever a roadblock, if there's ever a question, just reach out to me directly. You're going to receive a number of free resources from this book (valued at over $675.97!). All you have to do is go to www.FastLaunchCoach.com and download them. Plus, you'll be able to join my community and get answers to your challenges.

If you have interest in being one of my Private Clients – helping you generate six or even seven figures in recurring revenue – shoot me an email at scott@membershipmultipliers.com. Put in the subject line, *private client*, and let's have a conversation.

Listen, I want to do everything I can to help you continue to grow and impact more people. When I help you get **more** members and serve more people, that's how I'm leveraging **my** *why,* by leveraging my wisdom and knowledge **rather than** youth and energy. When you are able to help more people, I vicariously get to help those people, too.

There's an opportunity for me to come alongside you, to take the next step with you, and to help you fulfill your purpose. Shoot me an email and let's have the conversation.

I look forward to great things taking place in your life and business!

You're going to launch.

You have the tools necessary. Now go get more members and serve more people.

Go make it happen!

# ACKNOWLEDGMENTS

To sell anything you must have a strong and positive belief in yourself. To sell a "high-ticket membership offer" you must have extreme confidence in the outcome that your member can achieve. Personally, this would not be possible without the belief and confidence that my wife Kelly has continually instilled within me. Much of what has been shared in this book started with her belief in me.

To Mackenzie and Emily, I've carried many titles in this world, but being your dad is one of the greatest of all. One of the greatest joys your mom and I have is seeing you mature into the beautiful young women you are.

A very special thanks to my friend Kim Walsh Phillips who has been a constant encouragement and has helped outline the F.A.S.T. framework. I'm grateful for your friendship and the many ways you have helped me to help others.

A special thanks to Demi Stevens for your editorial genius, design, and guidance through this publishing process. Thanks for giving these words life and just making it all sound good. HA!

I'm also grateful for Jack Turk who helped compile this book and took hours of research, transcripts, and outlines and kicked off the writing process of bringing this work to life.

Finally, I'm grateful to my God who has brought me on this journey of faith. Much of what I've learned has come from being a member of what I consider to be the oldest and greatest membership of all-time – the local Church. To all my Pastor friends, know that you are leading the greatest membership organization in all the world. There is no other membership that has the eternal impact you're having.

# ABOUT THE AUTHOR

Scott Whitaker helps business coaches create, launch, and sell a high-ticket membership offer. He also provides services to help you and your coaches increase retention, create new membership levels and keep people from canceling their membership.

He is responsible for growing one of the largest membership organizations in its niche, taking it from just 72 members to over 3,127 members. And many of his clients have done the same.

Through his Seven Membership Multipliers, Scott helps membership businesses multiply and get to that next level of success, no matter where you are in the process. He offers limited VIP Power Days, Power Multipliers Club, Membership Maximizer, and Membership Accelerators Club. He is the founder of Membership Multipliers and the author of two books: *Accelerate: How to Get Your Next 10, 100, 500 or Even 1,000 Members* and *High-Ticket Coach: The F.A.S.T. System to Create, Launch and Sell a High-Ticket Membership Offer*.

www.FastLaunchCoach.com

www.MembershipMultipliers.com

www.Facebook.com/scottdwhitaker

www.LinkedIn.com/in/scott-whitaker

Made in the USA
Middletown, DE
24 April 2024

53444094R00116